Missoula
The Town and The People

by Betty Wetzel

with a chapter of geology
by Dave Alt

Photos by John Reddy
unless otherwise credited

published by
Montana Magazine
Helena, Montana 59604

William A. Cordingley, Chairman
Rick Graetz, President
Mark Thompson, Director of Publications
Carolyn Cunningham,
Editor— Montana Magazine
Barbara Fifer, Assistant Book Editor

About the Author

Betty Wetzel was born and raised in Roundup, where her father, A.W. Eiselein, founded and published the *Roundup Record-Tribune*. She graduated from the University of Montana in 1937. Wetzel had a major role in establishing the American branch of the British international development organization, Oxfam. She has written for Montana and national publications, lived and worked in Bangladesh for two years, and has held various other jobs. From 1960 to 1965, her husband, Dr. Winston W. Wetzel, was Superintendent of Missoula County High Schools. Two of their four children graduated from the University of Montana.

ISBN 0-938314-31-9 (P)
ISBN 0-938314-40-8 (H)
Published by Montana Magazine
© 1987 American Geographic Publishing • Box 5630 • Helena, MT 59604 • (406) 443-2842
Text © 1987 Betty Wetzel
Photos © 1987 John Reddy, unless otherwise indicated

Contents

	Acknowledgments	4
	Map	5
1	The Valley Dimension	6
2	Those People Received Us Friendly	10
3	Lumberjack Country	16
4	Eye of the Economy	26
5	Mr. Missoula	32
6	The University	40
7	Author, Author	48
8	Doers	54
9	Hospital Wars	62
10	Amenities	68
11	Liberal Arts	72
12	Geology	80

Front cover: Top, Missoula from Lincoln Hills. Left: Brooks Street; center, Snowbowl (COURTESY SNOWBOWL); *right, "The Griz," U of M campus.*
Back cover: left, Rattlesnake Creek; right, Missoula from the South Hills.

Clockwise from below: Annick Smith, U of M's Science Complex, in the Bitterroots, Pattee Canyon bike race.

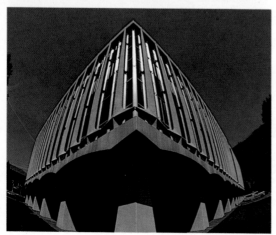

Acknowledgments

The author is indebted to Dr. Tom Paine, Arnold and Helen Bolle, and James and Jane Dew for pointing her in interesting directions, and to Maxine C. Johnson, director of the Bureau of Business and Economic Research, University of Montana, Missoula, for help in exploring Missoula's economy.

Above: Wilma building; left top: on Lolo Pass; right top: Sports Medicine center.

4

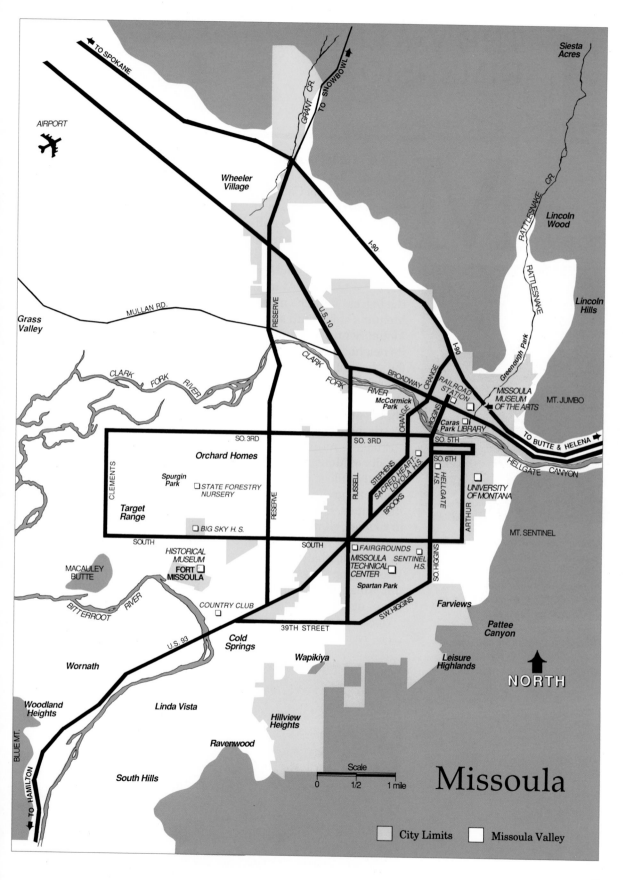

Missoula

Scale
0   1/2   1 mile

City Limits   Missoula Valley

1 THE VALLEY DIMENSION

Missoula is at its best in October. Mist rises from the Clark Fork of the Columbia River and the pervasive, if faint, odor of the pulp mill upwind at Frenchtown mingles with the smell of fallen leaves. Mount Lolo to the southwest is frosted with snow. At night, the biggest hunter's moon in Montana shines full above Mount Sentinel. Mount Jumbo, its neighbor, furnishes pasture for a herd of elk. Hungry black bears, storing up fat for the winter, are a pest in the orchards and garbage cans up Rattlesnake Creek.

Students return to the University of Montana, said to be the only college in the United States to have a mountain on its campus. Hikers, singly or in couples, climb the zig-zag path to the "M." Saturdays, there are football games at Washington-Grizzly stadium. An air of anticipation hangs over the Garden City.

Duck and pheasant season has already begun and hunters are sighting in their rifles for the big-game season opening soon. Canoes, having been mounted all summer on the road-worn pickups and cars of fishermen and hikers, are due to come down and be replaced by skis.

Missoula is addictive. It inspires a peculiar possessiveness in those who live here. Former University of Montana professor Leslie Fiedler, on returning to Missoula from the east and overhearing a fellow plane passenger observe, "Those are the Rocky Mountains," reacted with disdain, thinking that those weren't the Rocky Mountains, but the *Bitterroot* Mountains. And they were *his* mountains.

Harold Urey, the Nobel prize-

Above: Town and country are fast friends in Missoula. Wetting a line in the very heart of town from Higgins Avenue bridge.
Top: Lolo Peak, south of town in the Bitterroot Range.
GEORGE WUERTHNER PHOTO
Bottom: Late summer blooms in the Garden City at the western edge of the downtown area.

winning physicist, standing in the University Oval on the occasion of his 50th class reunion, exclaimed, "God, how I love this place!"

Here's how Elizabeth Savage's 1977 novel, *The Girls from the Five Great Valleys,* described it: "...the Missoula Valley is not level ground but a scoop in the Rocky Mountains that counts as its own Mounts Jumbo, Sentinel, even Lolo, just across the ridge...

"The Garden City where the Five Great Valleys meet: the Mission, the Missoula, the Blackfoot, the Hellgate, and the Bitterroot...

"Nobody comes from Missoula. Missoula is too new for people to come from. Missoula is a place that people come to...

"...in those days [the 1930s] the state belonged to those who lived there and the kids who went to the State University came from the state."

Her husband, Tom Savage, a University of Montana graduate, wrote in his novel, *I Heard My Sister Speak My Name:* "...Missoula, Montana, a small city but big for Montana, one with a certain style

St. Francis Xavier church, built in 1889, is a classic of its type and a Missoula landmark.

because the university is located there. A professor in Harris tweed with patches at the elbows is as likely to be abroad in the sunny city streets as a cowboy or sheep-herder from the surrounding hills and valleys. Books are read and even written there."

Norman Maclean, whose father was the Presbyterian minister in Missoula early in the century, wrote in his classic _A River Runs Through It:_ "Painted on one side of our Sunday school wall were the words, God Is Love. We always assumed that these three words were spoken directly to the four of us in our family and had no reference to the world outside, which my brother and I soon discovered was full of bastards, the number increasing rapidly the farther one gets from Missoula, Montana."

Another Montanan, John K. Hutchens, tells in _One Man's Montana_ of the Missoula of his youth: "The air smelled sweetly of pine. On the warmest day, sweat dried quickly in the clear, high air. The day ran long into the late, splendid sunset; at nine

o'clock of a summer evening a boy could read a book under the open sky. The nights were unfailingly cool. Everything about this town seemed large, perhaps because every street had mountains or prairie at its end. There was the feeling of big events, in the past or to come. Nature, huge and sometimes ominous, was just outside the door."

The Indians had detected an ominous presence here long before Hutchens' time. They named it "Lmisuletiku," which has been shortened to "Missoula." "I-sul" is a Sal-ish word meaning cold, either from lack of heat or from fear

or surprise. "Etiku" is water. The full meaning, "at the stream or water of surprise," was appropriate for Hellgate Canyon, where the Salish could expect to be ambushed by the Blackfeet as they made their way east of the mountains to hunt buffalo.

To a freshman coming to the university from east of the mountains in the dried-out 1930s or even today, when most years east of the mountains are reliably dry, the name still fits. A kid from a ranch near Circle or Big Sandy experiences a kind of claustrophobia when sur-rounded by western Mon-tana's hovering mountains. The state's famous "big sky" does not apply to Missoula, where its scope is consider-ably diminished by moun-tains and its blue all but obliterated by the air pollution typical of mountain valleys. It takes a while to be weaned from the wide-open spaces and the brilliant sunsets of the prairie. The valley seems like a remote, beautiful, imaginary place where life takes on a new dimension.

McCormick Park, part of a new riverfront park system.

Facing page: The mature core of Missoula, seen here from Leisure Highlands looking north across downtown.

8

2 THOSE PEOPLE RECEIVED US FRIENDLY

It is estimated that when Lewis and Clark entered Montana in 1805 there may have been 125,000 Indians on the Great Plains. No one knows how many of these earliest Americans lived in Montana, because all were nomadic buffalo hunters.

The Indians of the Missoula and Bitterroot valleys called themselves Salish, which means "the people." White men named them "the Flatheads" inaccurately and for reasons lost in the mists of the past.

The Salish were different from the Indians of the plains. Dr. Harry H. Turney-High, a professor of anthropology at the University of Montana in the 1930s, believed they had come from the upper Klamath region in Oregon and were descendants of the Semte'use. Their ancestors had drifted east of the Rockies and developed a taste for buffalo rather than fish. (Another food that became a favorite was the root of the bitterroot, dug in the Missoula and Bitterroot valleys before their blossoms opened in the spring.) After the 17th century, Blackfeet and Shoshone people (themselves being pushed ahead of white settlement) drove the Salish west of the Rockies, into the area of today's Missoula.

Dr. Turney-High, considered an authority on Montana Indian tribes, said of the Salish: "With the exception of the cruel treatment of their prisoners (which as it is general...must not be imputed to them as a particular vice) they had fewer failings than any of the tribes I ever met with. They were honest in their dealings, brave in the field, quiet and amenable to their chiefs, fond of cleanliness, and decided enemies of falsehood of every description. The

Salish-speaking people, related to tribes of the Columbia Plateau, inhabited the Missoula area until resettled to the St. Ignatius area by an 1855 treaty. 1915 POSTCARD COURTESY OF LEN ECKEL

A band of Flatheads under Chief Charlo remained in the Bitterroot Valley until the 1890s. Lolo Pass, shown here, was the site of a military stand-off when Chief Joseph, who hoped for help from the Flatheads, fled Idaho in 1877.

women are excellent wives and mothers...laziness was a stranger among them."

The mortal enemies of the Salish were the Blackfeet, who claimed the buffalo hunting grounds east of the mountains. They defended their right with guns obtained from northern and eastern fur trading posts while the Salish fought with bows and arrows. If it had not been for the battle skills of their chiefs, the bravery of their men and the excellence of their horses, the Salish would have been badly outclassed. Allies such as the Nez Perce assisted in forays onto the plains; early whites would be welcomed as other potential allies.

When the Lewis and Clark Expedition entered the Bitterroot Valley on September 4, 1805, and met a party of 400 Salish, Capt. William Clark wrote in his journal: "Those people received us friendly, threw white robes over our Shoulders and Smoked in the pipes of peace..."

The members of the expedition were the first white men ever encountered by the Salish, who thought they must

Ranch west of Lolo.

11

LOLO SUMMIT

THE LEWIS AND CLARK PARTY CROSSED THIS
PASS SEPT. 13, 1805, WESTBOUND FOR THE
PACIFIC AFTER A LONG DETOUR TO THE SOUTH.

From the headwaters of the Missouri they had crossed the
mountains to the Salmon. Finding that river impassable, they
traded for packhorses, hired an Indian guide, and
came north to an Indian trail across the
mountains here. Tired and ill-fed, the men were
to have a hard struggle in early snow along the
steep ridges which the trail followed for most
of its 125 mile course west to the
Clearwater River.

247

12

*Left: On the Lewis and Clark Trail.
Bottom: Fort Missoula was mostly
a sleepy frontier post. An excellent
historical museum has developed
here. Facing page: Rock Creek—
30 minutes from town, blue-rib-
bon–class fishing.*

have been robbed since they wore no blankets, according to an Indian girl named Agnes, who later became the second wife of Chief Victor. York, Clark's black servant, struck fear into the Indians who darkened their faces only when they went on the warpath.

After exchanging seven of their footsore horses for seven "ellegant" Salish horses, Lewis and Clark moved on to where the town of Lolo is today. A historical marker commemorates the camp which they called "Traveller's Rest." Warned by Toby, their Indian guide, of the ordeal that lay ahead in crossing Lolo Pass, they paused for three days to repack their gear, repair their moccasins and feed their horses.

There are conflicting stories as to the origin of the name "Lolo." One is that Toby could not pronounce "w" and called Captain Lewis "Lolo." Some say it is a corruption of the French name "LeLouis,"

and also honors the captain. Others say that it was named for a mixed-blood trapper named Lawrence Rence who lived on the creek and was called "Lou-Lou" by the Indians, who could not pronounce the letter "r."

It took the expedition 11 days in late September to cross what they called "these most terrible mountains," battling snow, bitter cold, hunger and exhaustion. Lolo Pass proved the cruelest test of the whole two-year journey.

Inspired by the 19th-century doctrine of Manifest Destiny, settlers arrived shortly thereafter. The valley's first permanent white resident is thought to have been David Pattee, who moved from the Bitterroot to the Missoula Valley in 1858 to farm in what is now called Pattee Canyon, south of Missoula.

In the same

year William T. Hamilton and a mixed-blood named McKay— two army scouts from Fort Walla Walla—camped at the junction of Rattlesnake Creek and the Clark Fork River. Hamilton, noticing that Indian trails from all the adjoining valleys converged here, thought it a good spot for a trading post. He returned to build a two-room log cabin, where he sold whiskey, the basic commodity of most early-day Montana trading posts.

Joining David Pattee to farm the fertile, well-watered valley with its protective mountains and temperate climate were Robert Pelkey, who brought his family from St. Louis, Missouri, and Captain Richard Grant, formerly an officer with the Hudson's Bay Company. They settled near Grant Creek. French Canadians Baptiste Du Charme and Louis Brun (Brown) settled to the north and were soon joined by other Frenchmen, beginning the French community whose influence still can be seen in

Missoula. Frenchtown was established in 1864.

When the Mullan Road from Walla Walla to Fort Benton was built in 1859-60 at a cost of $230,000, the tiny settlement had its first tenuous link to the outside world. The 50 miles of road through the Missoula Valley forded the Clark Fork River eleven times. Six years after its completion, it was estimated that 20,000 emigrants and $1 million worth of freight had passed over it.

Among the first to take advantage of the new military road were Christopher Higgins and Francis Lyman Worden, who reached Hellgate in 1860 with a pack train of 76 animals loaded with merchandise and a safe with walls of steel five inches thick. The success of their trading post was already assured.

Part of Washington Territory since its creation in 1853, and of Idaho Territory since 1863, the Missoula settlement became part of Montana Territory when the latter was created on May 26, 1864.

Fort Missoula was established in 1877, in response to fears that the settlers were without protection should the Flathead Indians turn hostile. But construction had hardly begun before its soldiers were dispatched to halt the advance of a band of Nez Perce Indians led by Chief Joseph

Fourteen years previously, these Nez Perce had refused to move onto an Idaho reservation, guaranteed to them in an 1855 treaty, from their land in northeastern Oregon. (Gold had been discovered almost in the center of their homeland.) In the summer of 1877, they were obeying a deadline to move onto that reservation when some young warriors killed white settlers. The entire band fled for Can-

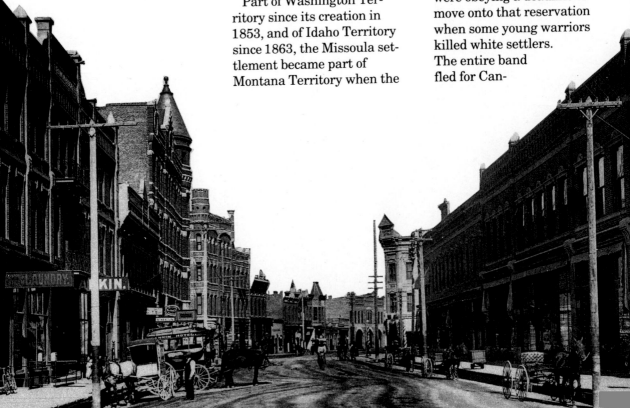

ada, intending to move peacefully across Montana. They were pursued by U.S. troops under the command of General O.O. Howard.

The soldiers from Fort Missoula, assisted by hastily recruited volunteers, threw up log fortifications across the Lolo Trail. They failed to deter the Nez Perce, who left campfires burning during the night and proceeded south around the sleeping soldiers to the Bitterroot Valley. Derisive settlers labeled the effort "Fort Fizzle."

One of the last Indian battles in the United States was the Battle of the Big Hole, fought fewer than a hundred miles from Missoula. Here 30 civilians, and 146 soldiers from Fort Missoula led by Colonel Gibbon and 15 officers, attacked the Indians. After a brutal fight from August 9 to August 11, 15 warriors remained behind, firing occasional volleys while the rest of the band and their horses resumed the flight north. Chief Joseph's little band surrendered to General Nelson A. Miles on October 5, 1877, after a five-day battle fought in a blizzard near the Bearpaw Mountains, only about 50 miles from the Canadian border.

Today it is estimated that there are about 3,500 Native Americans living in Missoula County. Many of the descendants of those Salish people who had received Lewis and Clark "friendly" live on the Flathead Reservation in neighboring Lake County.

25 DOLLARS FINE
FOR RIDING OR DRIVING OVER THIS
BRIDGE FASTER THAN A WALK.

15

3 LUMBERJACK COUNTRY

Historically and geographically, Missoula shares little with the rest of Montana. Ten to 20 thousand or so years ago, the valley was at the bottom of a huge lake whose waters had risen and fallen over the millennia, leaving the marks of its ancient shorelines on the sides of Mts. Sentinel and Jumbo. The lake eventually destroyed the ice dam that had created it, spilling along the bed of the Clark Fork River.

The Missoula area was not part of Montana's "fur frontier." The free trappers who came south from Canada or up the Missouri River to barter for beaver pelts with the Indians, did much trading on the tributaries of the Missouri. After 1846, Fort Benton was headquarters for Montana's fur trade and the pelts were shipped down the Missouri to St. Louis.

Missoula was not seriously afflicted with "gold fever," although Montana's first gold strike was fewer than 60 miles away at Gold Creek, a branch of the Hellgate River (now the Clark Fork), in 1852. Bannack, Virginia City and Last Chance Gulch (Helena) attracted hordes of prospectors and produced about $90 million worth of gold between 1862 and 1876.

Cowboys ranged east of the mountains. Missoula never knew the likes of "Teddy Blue" Abbott, who trailed longhorn cattle from Fort-Worth, Texas, to Miles City in the days of the open range. Nor does it remember the fabled Hard Winter of 1886-87, when probably 60 percent of the territory's cattle was lost.

Early in the 20th century, railroad man Jim Hill had a vision of a farm family on every 160 or 320 acres of public domain along Montana's hi-

Facing page: Tamaracks of the Bitterroot Mountains in fall colors. Below: Logs at decking area of Champion International mill east of Missoula.

pany was already established by Eddy, Hammond and Company. C.H. McLeod arrived from New Brunswick to begin his 60-year management of "The Merc" in 1880. The *Missoulian* was established as a weekly newspaper in 1873.

After the Northern Pacific Railroad expanded into the Missoula valley in 1883, there was need for a larger sawmill to supply lumber for the railroad, and the settlers it brought with it. A.B. Hammond built the Big Blackfoot Lumber Company at Bonner at a cost of half a million dollars. It was said to be the best and biggest sawmill in the world.

In 1898 Marcus Daly's Anaconda Mining Company bought the Bonner sawmill and its timberlands from Hammond to assure the production of props and timbers for the tunnels of the Butte mines.

Missoula was the hub of Montana's timber industry.

line, to be transported, together with land speculators, on Hill's Great Northern Railroad. This "homestead boom" was not heard in Missoula, nor was the "bust" that followed when, from 1921 to 1925, one out of every two Montana farmers lost his place by mortgage foreclosure. Few "Honyockers" got as far west as Missoula.

The city west of the plains had its own history; its destiny lay in its forests. Hellgate was named the seat of Missoula County when Montana Territory was created on May 26, 1864. In November of that year C.P. Hig-

gins, Frank Worden and David Pattee formed the Missoula Mills Company and built a sawmill four miles up the Clark Fork from Hellgate on Rattlesnake Creek, the present site of Missoula.

By 1873 the Missoula National Bank, with capital stock of $50,000, opened in the back of the general store of Worden and Company, and Missoula was in business. The Missoula National became the First National Bank, and moved to its present location on the corner of Higgins Avenue and Front Street in 1889. The forerunner of the Missoula Mercantile Com-

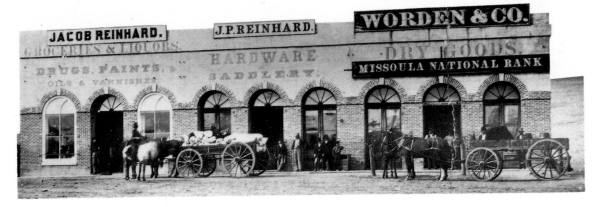

In addition to Bonner and the Western Lumber Company at Milltown, smaller mills were operated by enterprising loggers throughout the area.

As the years went on, Missoula was sustained by what seemed an inexhaustible supply of timber and a stable market. Its early years as a logging headquarters were probably as violent and colorful as the more popularized doings at mining camps and cow towns. The roistering of lumberjacks, charging into Missoula after a spring "drive" of logs down the Clearwater and Blackfoot rivers from Seeley Lake, was something to behold. Following a winter of isolation in snowy woods, with no whiskey, no women, no comforts and no entertainment, they vented their pent-up energy at the saloons and hurdy-gurdy houses of Bonner and Missoula.

Shortly after the turn of the century, in 1908, the United States Forest Service established its regional head- quarters at Missoula. The School of Forestry at the University of Montana became a center for forest and game management research, as well as for the training of generations of state and regional foresters. Smokejumper training began experimentally near here in 1939, became operational in 1940, and the world-famous Aerial Fire Depot was built in 1954.

The wood products industry remains Missoula's major employer. In 1984 loggers and workers in saw- mills,

19

Blue Mountain lookout tower.

plywood plants, the pulp and paper plant and other wood-related firms earned about $92.7 million, which accounted for about 38 percent of the area's export industries. When the thousand or so resource managers employed by the U.S. Forest Service, the U.S. Bureau of Land Management, and the Montana Division of Forestry are added, with their salaries of some $26 million, the total accounts for about $118.7 million a year, or almost half of Missoula's economic base.

Today's efficient, highly mechanized logger, with his chain saw, winches and self-loading truck, barely resembles the turn-of-the century "bull of the woods," who could manhandle a "drive" of giant logs from Seeley Lake to Bonner, using only an axe, saw, peavey and horse-drawn sleigh.

Champion International, the nation's fourth largest forest products company, with headquarters in Stamford, Connecticut, has 400 locations nationwide. Missoula is one of them. In 1977 Champion took over the forest resources and

Champion International has a mill in Missoula. Most of its resource is small-diameter logs—the old growth is about gone.

operations formerly owned by the Anaconda Company and Hoerner Waldorf. Its investment in Montana is substantial, including 683,000 acres of timberlands, several sawmills producing a wide variety of lumber products and the plywood plant at Bonner.

There is considerable apprehension among Missoula's working people and business community about possible plant closures or cutbacks. Champion International's approximately 1,500 employees have reluctantly signed a contract calling for 11 percent to 13 percent reductions in compensation and benefits. Champion no longer does its own logging and trucking, contracting with "gypo loggers" (independent operators) to deliver logs to its mills.

Logging interests and environmentalists argue over whether the supply of timber in western Montana can be sustained. The hard fact is that it takes 120 years for a tree in Montana to become a saw log, compared with only 40 years for a tree growing along the west coast. Today most of the Montana cut is less than

Champion's plywood plant at Bonner.

complains that, while studies of public land use (Roadless Area Review and Evaluation, called RARE I and II) have gone on for 19 years, "Mother Nature has continued to produce trees." He adds that lumber prices have been low and, with Canada supplying 31 percent of the U.S. lumber market, "there is a lot of uncertainty in the industry."

The original stands of large-diameter timber, logged by the Anaconda Company since 1882, are gone. The few remaining "old-growth" trees are hard to reach. Only one Champion International mill is still equipped to handle large logs. The company cannot compete in particle board construction but continues to modernize its plywood plants in Bonner and Libby.

Engineering studies are now being made to determine whether Champion International will modernize its present, outmoded Montana plants or build a completely new, highly mechanized, small-log mill in the Missoula area. This is both good news and bad news because employment would likely decline sub-

12" in diameter. Should the slow-growing trees on Montana's public lands and national forests be harvested, and, if so, how?

Dr. Arnold W. Bolle, long-time dean of the university's School of Forestry, has been a foe of "timber mining." He advocates the type of forest management that will maintain production for the future.

Bob Kelley, Public Affairs Manager of Champion's Missoula operations until March 1986, is forthright. He

Facing page: Bonner, a "company town" under the Anaconda Company's regime, is a hard-working satellite of Missoula.

stantially in either case.

"To provide more stability to the local economy," Kelley says, "we must examine the potential of adding value to our products instead of just shipping raw materials. We could construct window frames, doors, truck beds, furniture, and dozens of other products." It is Kelley's opinion that "the worst sin any company can have is not to make a profit. You can't employ people or support a community by your contributions if you aren't showing a profit."

Bob Kelley is not a typical spokesman for corporate America. An Anaconda Irishman whose father worked in the smelter, and whose Irish-immigrant grandfather had a price on his head for organizing a union in the Cripple Creek, Colorado, mine fields, Kelley has a deep understanding of Montana's economic problems. He is also equipped to deal with them.

A graduate of the University of Montana in biological sciences, he earned a graduate degree in environmental

engineering at the University of Minnesota. He has worked as an environmental aide to Senator William Proxmire and former Montana Congressman Dick Shoup. He has also managed a private consulting firm specializing in environmental impact statements, in Washington, D.C., and New York City. Here is how he views the Montana economy:

"I hear people saying that we ought to bring high-tech industries here—have another Silicon Valley. We have to get our priorities in order as to

what we have to offer and how we can best take advantage of our opportunities. We don't have an M.I.T. or Stanford here. Montana and its people have spent more time arguing with each other about what they can and can't do with a resource while the rest of the world has passed us by. We have our own civil war going on here. I am basically an optimist and I don't think that we should sit around worrying about what we don't have. Let's get together and join hands and decide what we can have."

The Stone Container Corporation pulp mill at Frenchtown is a stabilizing force in the Missoula economy. Its jobs have the highest pay scale. The median wage (half the salaries are above this and half below) was $37,500 in 1984, at which time the mill had 739 employees, for a total payroll of $27,661,000. It was one of the few industries in Missoula County to experience an increase in labor income between 1979 and 1984.

Nearly all of Montana's timber goes to mills producing lumber and plywood, but less than half of the wood fiber in the timber is actually used. Much of the scrap wood and sawdust that formerly went up in smoke to become a source of air and water pollution is today trucked or shipped by rail to Frenchtown's pulp and paper mill.

Built in 1957 as a joint venture between Waldorf Paper Products and Hoerner Boxes to produce pulp for midwest plants, the mill began producing paper in 1960. It merged with Champion International in 1977, and was sold by Champion to Stone Container Corporation in 1986. The Frenchtown mill is not expected to expand its facilities or production.

It currently produces a kraft paper known as linerboard, used in the manufacture of corrugated containers. Frenchtown is one of the largest linerboard facilities in the U.S., having the capacity to produce 1,850 tons per day.

During its early days, the Frenchtown pulp mill, upwind from Missoula, blanketed the city with emissions from its smokestacks which, combined with temperature inversions in the valley, made for intolerable air pollution. Offended citizens were further enraged when they complained about the stink and were told by some businessmen, "It may be stink to you, but it smells like money to me."

Over the years, with the addition of scrubbers and the scientific recovery of chemicals used in the pulping process, the odor and pollution have been reduced considerably. Currently, the mill meets both state and federal environmental standards. Treatment of effluents discharged into the Clark Fork River remains a major concern of area residents.

"We want to be good citizens," says Daniel T. Potts, manager of the Frenchtown

Stone Container Corporation, formerly owned by Champion and before that by Hoerner Waldorf, is one of the U.S.'s largest manufacturers of liner board for construction of corrugated cardboard. Pattern in the foreground is wastewater aeration treatment.

mill. "It just makes good sense if we want to stay in business and be successful."

Potts appears to be just that, a good citizen who personally serves on various community boards. He's opposed to air pollution (he runs five miles every morning). Eminently well qualified for his job, with a degree in chemical engineering from the University of Washington plus an MBA from Stanford, he has worked for Weyerhaeuser, Hoerner Waldorf and Champion International in various capacities around the country. He has been at the Frenchtown plant for a total of eight years and has been manager for the past three.

Potts and Bob Kelley represent the modern approach to wood products, still the backbone of Missoula's economy. The days of the "bull of the woods" are long gone.

4 EYE OF THE ECONOMY

This book is about Missoula today. It is about people who were born here and people who have only recently arrived. It is about people who want to stay here. And it is about native sons and daughters who would like to return, and are returning in increasing numbers.

Missoula lies at the heart of some of the grandest country on the continent. As with most of the mountain west, the area's inaccessibility and self-protecting Indian residents prevented "the States" from knowing it existed just 125 years ago. Then, isolation and distance were curses. Today, not much more than a century after the white folks came, Americans are hungering for what this part of Montana has in more abundance than almost any other place in the nation—unspoiled, natural beauty, wilderness at its doorstep in every direction: Anaconda/Pintler, 158,516 acres; Bob Marshall, 1,009,356 acres; Great Bear, 286,700 acres; Mission Mountain, 73,877 acres; Rattlesnake, 33,000 acres; Scapegoat, 239,936, acres; Selway-Bitterroot, 1,340,681 acres; Welcome Creek, 28,135 acres.

Missoula-area residents, plus their automobile exhaust, wood-burning stoves and aerosol spray cans, to say nothing of the up-wind pulp mill and unavoidable temperature inversions in the deep valley, have made winter air pollution a scandal. If Missoula lacks fresh air in the winter, however, the 3,170,207 acres of adjoining wilderness has plenty of it.

One absent from the city for 20 years wants to know who lives in all the new houses that crawl up and around the mountains and into the

Right: The fog from Hillview Heights.
Bottom: Missoula from Blue Mountain, southwest of town.

adjoining valleys. The now-solidly-packed "Farviews" runs into something called "South Hills" and proceeds up the Bitterroot Valley. Pattee Canyon, where a few folks used to isolate themselves and young lovers parked, now looks like suburbia. North of town, elegant, landscaped homes

The Rattlesnake Creek area under the west face of Mount Jumbo, which wears an "L" for Loyola High School.

now preside over the formerly unlandscaped and dusty Rattlesnake Creek area. Orchard Homes, a haven for rural folks who gardened in its loamy soil and where Missoulians could be assured of fresh-picked sweet corn or pick-your-own strawberries and raspberries at summer's peak, is jammed with rows of mobile homes that stretch beyond the Clark Fork and out toward Mullan Road.

According to the 1980 census, 33,000 now live in the city limits (almost all the above developments excluded), an increase of 6,000 above the 1960 census. The Chamber of Commerce claims 68,000 in the "metropolitan area," encompassing 12.9 square miles. Missoula County added 31,000 residents from 1960 to 1980 and in 1985 had a population estimated at 77,300. Missoula County's population increased 30 percent from 1970 to 1980.

Recession hit Missoula in 1980, when reorganization of the Burlington Northern Railroad caused a loss of permanent jobs. (Between 1979 and 1984, Missoula County lost $8 million a year in labor income from railroads.) More jobs were lost by a decline in the wood products industry, closure of the Van Evans plywood plant, and increased labor productivity in the remaining facilities. Population growth from 1980 to 1985 was only 600.

Nevertheless, Missoula has more than doubled its population in the past 20 years. What do all these Missoulians do? As stated, half have found jobs in the wood products and paper industries or the federal and state agencies that manage timber resources. Other federal employees work at the U.S. Post Office, the Internal Revenue Service and other agencies, and earn about $38.9 million a year.

Surprisingly, motor carriers and the University of Montana are tied for third place among Missoula's basic industries. In 1984 each had a payroll of about $30 million.

Missoula's trucking industry hauls raw materials, primarily logs, to Missoula and finished products to market. Trucks bring consumer goods to Missoula residents. But most important, Missoula-based trucks transport goods throughout the U.S. They neither originate nor terminate in Missoula. These operations have an impact on the local economy because several company headquarters are located here and many drivers live here. Missoula is located on east-west Interstate 90 and only about a hundred miles west of its junction with north-south I-15. Taken together, the wage and salary workers plus the self-employed truckers earned about $31.2 million in 1984 and represented about 12.7 percent of

From Bass Creek Road looking to the rugged Bitterroot Mountains.

the total labor income for all basic industries.

The $30.1 million of labor income generated by the University of Montana represents the earnings of all university employees—faculty, staff and students—and accounts for about 12.3 percent of Missoula's economic base.

In Missoula, retail trade, professional and medical services are the most important trade industries. Wholesale and retail trade, service and certain financial businesses generate labor income of about $21 million, or about 8.6 percent of the total.

Miscellaneous manufacturing, such as a dental-instrument maker and a manufacturer of canvas products, add about $7.8 million, 3.2 percent of the total. The area's farms and ranches, plus several mines and the firms servicing them, generate about $4.6 million, or 1.9 percent.

It's difficult to measure how

much the tourism industry contributes to Missoula's economy. Purchases of food, gasoline and other consumer items are not segregated between residents and nonresidents. Workers in lodging places, a known component of the tourism industry, earned about $4.6 million, or about 1.9 percent. In 1982, Missoula County ranked seventh among the state's 56 counties in terms of labor income generated by motel and hotel employment. With more than 1,300 travel-related jobs, Missoula County ranks sixth in total travel employment.

Total labor income for Missoula's basic industries in 1984 was about $244.9 million, down about 6.4 percent from $261.7 million in 1979. Per

capita income for the county in 1984 was about $10,600, slightly below the Montana average.

That's how most people earn their livings in Missoula. But the number of dollars generated by commerce doesn't begin to explain the motivation behind the busy lives of the 68,000 or so people who live here.

Fly fishing was a favorite sport of Presidents Eisenhower, Hoover and Coolidge, to say nothing of the likes of Ernest Hemingway and Andrew Carnegie. It is also a favorite pastime of Missoula's loggers, truck drivers, university professors, physicians and retail store clerks who give credence to the claim of the state's recent business re-

Above left: "Downtown"—Higgins Avenue, the old shopping, finance and trade center.
Above right: '80s style—the Southgate Mall.
Left: Orchard Homes area—indeed it once was dominated by apple orchards.

cruitment advertising campaign: "It's always Friday in Montana." A few miles in the old pickup, a short hike or a paddle in a canoe promises Missoula fishers an isolated spot on a lake, river or creek with good prospects, depending on skill and conditions, of a catch of rainbow, cutthroat, brown, brook or Dolly Varden trout.

Hand-tied flies are luring more than trout these days. According to the *Wall Street Journal,* fly fishing has become the "in" sport of yuppies and business executives, who are said to be fishing in designer waders. There are reportedly about a million people fly fishing, up 25 percent from five years ago. But so far, Missoula anglers have not noticed the influx and are not standing

This is why they all try to stay in Missoula.
Above: On Rock Creek.
Right top: Clear summer skies are for all the birds.
Right center: Popular with floaters and fishermen alike, the Blackfoot River keeps on rollin'.

shoulder-to-shoulder on the banks of the Blackfoot, Clark Fork or any of several hundred favorite fishing holes, the exact locations of which are closely-held secrets.

Bicycling also is big in

Left: Doing an "endo" in the Alberton Gorge on the Clark Fork River. GEORGE WUERTHNER

Missoula. According to Mary Cheryl Larango of the city's bicycle program, "In terms of activities, bicycling is outranked only by walking or hiking and picnicking. We have almost a 60 percent ridership in Missoula." Missoula is headquarters for several major cycling events, including the annual Tour of the Swan River Valley and the Western Montana Hill Climb Championship.

And on any warm weekend afternoon during the summer, up to a dozen hang gliders take off from the top of Mount Sentinel for a lofty ride over the Garden City.

Missoulians of whatever persuasion can take advantage of Montana's premier urban wilderness by driving or biking four miles north on Van Buren Street and Rattlesnake Drive to the trailhead of the Rattlesnake National Recreation Area and Wilderness. It is the only wilderness in Montana, or perhaps the nation, that literally touches the outskirts of a city.

Closed to motorized vehicles and dogs, the wilderness is a place for elk, white-tailed and mule deer, mountain lions, black bears, day hikers, picnickers and horseback riders, as well as anglers and cross-country skiers. Any and all can savor this most accessible 33,000-acre wilderness.

In Missoula, there's no excuse for winter ennui. Take skiing, for instance. Missoula's Snow Bowl, just a 20-minute drive northwest of town, has the longest vertical drop in Montana and a groomed intermediate trail more than three miles long. Snow Bowl has two double chair lifts, a T-bar and rope tow, plus warming huts, a cafeteria and saloon.

Marshall Ski Area, seven miles east of Missoula, features family skiing on its eight miles of slopes and trails. It has a triple chairlift, as well as T-bar and rope tow. The whole hill can be rented for a party of night skiing.

Thousands of miles of nearby forest roads and marked trails are available for cross-country skiing and snowmobiling.

Winter or summer, spring or fall, Missoula provides the kind of outdoor recreation opportunities that keep visitors visiting and residents happy.

5 MR. MISSOULA

The home of Barbara and John Toole, high on the mountainside of Farviews, is situated so that most of the windows overlook the town. In the golden light of a mid-autumn afternoon, fall foliage gilds the street patterns of the Garden City below. Only a filmy mist hangs in the air, colored faintly apricot. Today there is no smog.

The greeting is warm, resuming friendships going back to university days, when Barbara was a classmate. Age has only enhanced her fresh-faced beauty.

Facing page: The former Milwaukee Railroad Station, now a social spot for dinner and drinks along the Clark Fork River's developing park system. Below: John Toole.

In the book-lined living room, over coffee, I explain that I am here to see "Mr. Missoula." That's what they call John Toole.

By the 1980s, the Garden City had suffered a mid-life crisis resulting from the deterioration of its once-proud and prosperous Higgins Avenue, and the uglification of the nearby banks of the Clark Fork River. The abandoned right-of-way of the Milwaukee Railroad, on the north bank, was weed-grown and depressing.

Seemingly overnight, Missoula was saved by civic vision and action. Its river banks became landscaped parklands and playing fields, and today the community reflects the elegant ambience of a European university town.

I asked a number of people how this had come about. The answer was, invariably, "Go see John Toole."

John Toole combines aesthetic sense with tenacity. He also has clout. He has no enemies and nobody can question his motives. For one thing, the Tooles were among the earliest white settlers. John told the

Missoula's water system is privately owned and operated and perhaps has been since the days when One-Eyed Riley and helper delivered. COURTESY MANSFIELD LIBRARY, UNIV. OF MONTANA

family story in his book, *The Baron, The Miner, The Logger and Me.* A successful businessman, now retired, he established and operated one of the city's leading insurance firms. He was vice president of the Constitutional Convention that rewrote Montana's constitution in 1964. (His grandfather, John R. Toole, had been a member of the state's 1889 Constitutional Convention.) His brother was the late K. Ross Toole, firebrand environmentalist and historian. John spoke for old-timers and new-timers. He is a Republican admired and respected as well by Democrats and young activists. If Missoula is the Athens of Montana, John is one of its philosopher-kings.

The refurbishing of center city started back in 1969 when John Toole was a member of the Park Board, and a flood

left an island in the river channel. The island was donated to the city. The north channel of the river was closed. Pooling of bond issues by Missoula County High School, the university and the city was necessary to secure the land up and down the river, which is now publicly owned.

Street closures and extensions were tied up in seemingly endless litigation. Every excavation in the city was tapped for fill and top soil. The Anaconda Company was

asked for, and donated, handsome turn-of-the-century streetlights from its closed smelter in Anaconda. Parking lots were built, along with a stairway leading up to Higgins Avenue.

James Caras, a Greek immigrant who had come to Missoula in 1908 and built a two-wheeled fruit cart into the town's most prosperous floral and landscaping business, sent the first check for $1,000. That started public monetary support. Banker Randy Jacobs sent an unsolicited check for $10,000. "Caras Park" on the north riverbank soon became a reality. It was all done by donated funds. The Sheraton Hotel was built on adjoining land as an extension of Missoula's downtown redevelopment.

After his service on the Park

The old Northern Pacific Railroad station (now Burlington Northern) at the north end of Higgins Avenue.

The spacious Orchard Homes and Target Range areas are growing, and are beyond the city limits and city services.

Board, John Toole was elected to the city council, serving from 1976 to 1984. He was mayor in 1984-85. He rails against the reluctance of business and professional people to run for public office or serve on important boards. The job of improving Missoula is never done, he explains.

It might have seemed easy early in the century when *The Daily Missoulian,* on Sunday, August 21, 1910, carried

the headline: "Building a Model System of Sewers that will Last Missoula for All Time." The *Missoulian* continued: "The mains [which emptied into the Clark Fork River] have been given size enough to carry all the flow that will come from the entire system, even to the extreme limits of the Rattlesnake valley and far out on the west side flat." There had been a "vexatious delay" caused by legal difficulties which "had been interposed by the state board of health in connection with the use of the Missoula river as a receptacle of the sewage." The 1910 editor of the *Missoulian* would be amazed at the development of "the extreme limits of the Rattlesnake valley." Dwellers in Missoula's most exclusive residential area

dump their sewage into septic systems. Jim Carlson, environmental specialist with the Missoula City-County Health Department, worries that the sewage goes straight through porous sands and gravels of the valley and winds up in Rattlesnake Creek, the groundwater, and ultimately, the Clark Fork River.

Not only the Rattlesnake, but Target Range and Orchard Homes have the same problem, as does nearby Frenchtown, where private wells have already become polluted. All Missoula-area water, whether from city mains or private wells, comes ultimately from groundwater. Until recent problems with the parasite *Giardia,* much of Missoula's water came directly from Rattlesnake Creek.

The Missoula water system is a problem. Dating back to about 1889, it was once owned by copper king W.A. Clark. The system passed into the hands of the Montana Power Co. in 1929, which sold it to an absentee landlord, Mountain Water, in 1979. The last of Missoula's wooden water mains installed at the turn of

Lincoln Hills "up the Rattlesnake," an exclusive new subdivision.

*Right: The pines and quiet
residential neighborhoods of the
Rattlesnake Creek area.
Below: Pattee Canyon, possessed
of larger properties and hardy
winter-time commutes.*

the century were removed or
bypassed in 1986.

A condemnation lawsuit
may eventually put the city
water system under public
ownership in the city's public
works department.

Then there's the problem of
air pollution. Missoula's location in a deep mountain valley
results in frequent wintertime
temperature inversions when
stagnant air hangs 500' to
1,200' above the valley floor.
The wood products industry
was largely responsible for
high particulate levels in the
air during the 1960s and early
1970s. In 1968 the Montana
Clean Air Act was passed, and
strict industrial emission standards followed. Missoula women formed an organization
called GASP—Gals Against
Smog and Pollution—and pic-
keted the Frenchtown pulp
mill and other sites. By 1974
industrial emissions in the
valley had been reduced by
more than 90 percent.

But in the mid-1970s, following the OPEC oil crisis and
an increase in the price of
natural gas, air pollution of-
ficials noticed a rise in pollution from wood smoke. Study

of emissions showed that wood-
burning accounted for 54 percent, while industry, road dust
and auto emissions were responsible for the rest.

In 1977 the Montana Legislature funded a statewide
study of air pollution. In 1978
and 1979, pulmonary function
tests were given to a sampling
of Missoula school children.
Comparisons showed that children in Great Falls consistently
exhibited better pulmonary
function than children from
urban Missoula. "Possibly

these changes are reversible
and short-term and may not
lead to significant permanent
lung damage....However, the
long-term effects are not
known, and the effects upon
the growing lungs of children
less than five or six years old
are unexplored," said the late
Dr. Kit Johnson, director of
the Montana Air Pollution
Study.

There is no doubt that high
pollutant levels make breath-
ing and other normal activities more difficult for those

*One of Missoula's biggest
bedroom communities is to the
south of town around Lolo.*

36

Pollution trapped by thermal inversions in Missoula's cozy valley has been a nagging development problem. The Stone Container plant's emissions have a lingering effect familiar to Missoulians. GEORGE WUERTHNER

suffering from asthma, chronic bronchitis, emphysema and other pulmonary diseases.

Citizen committees to study and make recommendations on Missoula's air quality suggested an expanded public education program to teach residents about the effects of wood smoke and techniques to reduce emissions. A system of voluntary discontinuance of wood burning during wintertime inversions is now in effect, together with a system of measuring air quality and alerting the public if air is "good," "moderate," "unhealthful," "very unhealthful," or "hazardous."

Missoula old-timers recall that air pollution is not a new problem in the valley. Temperature inversions have al-

ways existed. Before natural gas, all homes were heated by wood or coal stoves and furnaces, and smoke poured from the smokestacks of the Montana Power steam plant and the university heating plant. Five tepee burners spewed smoke and ash within the city limits and coal-fired steam engines huffed and puffed into the Northern Pacific stations. (The Milwaukee had been electrified early on.) Dust from unpaved streets and horse manure added to the particulate count in earlier times.

One of the main problems of Missoula is Missoula County. The city boundaries do not include all of Orchard Homes, Pattee Canyon, the Rattlesnake, Target Range or other adjoining or nearby develop-

ments that add to and confound such urban challenges as smog, traffic, and water and sewage problems. Residents of these outlying areas are reluctant to be included in the city limits because their taxes unquestionably would be raised. It has been suggested that the city of Missoula should simply disband and become part of Missoula County. It would then be run by the Missoula County Commissioners.

At this writing, Missoula is the only county in the United States to have an all-woman board of county commissioners. They are Ann Mary Dussault, Barbara Evans, and Janet Stevens. In addition to the commissioners, the county auditor, clerk and recorder, clerk of district court, personnel director, public defender, and superintendent of schools are also women.

Ann Mary Dussault became a Missoula County Commissioner after serving in the state legislature for eight years. During her last term she was House Majority Leader—the first woman of the state to serve in that capacity.

Historic Missoula County Court-house is decorated with original Paxson paintings of Lewis and Clark's progress. Behind is a more mundane, but modern addition.

(Her father, Edward Dussault, had been majority leader of the Senate.)

Ann Mary has a B.A. in music therapy from Michigan State University—hardly a preparation for a politician. Having a developmentally handicapped sister, she was always aware of the problems and care, or lack of care, of such citizens. Upon returning to Montana and discovering the state of affairs at the then State Home for the Retarded in Boulder, she was outraged.

She now recalls, "Somebody said to me, 'If you think it's so bad, why don't you do something about it?'"

"So I said, 'Watch this'."

That's when she ran and was elected to the legislature. After eight years, two as majority

leader, she suffered from "legislative burnout," and decided her state experience could be equally helpful in tackling the problems of Missoula County. The tall, attractive Ms. Dussault calls herself a "progressive cynic." She says that, "There are always a lot of roadblocks and nay-sayers, nothing will happen overnight, but Missoula is capable of controlling its own future."

She believes that the future lies in the development of "value added" industries like the Norco Manufacturing Company, which builds wooden school desks. But Missoula faces three or four years of insecurity before the effects of the Build Montana program or Community Development Block Grants are felt.

Describing her vision for Missoula's future, she says: "We need to create new jobs, train people to do these jobs and get them off public assistance."

Bradley Hurd, editor of the *Missoulian,* says "Missoula is a wonderful place to publish a newspaper. It is so diverse. All the different factions seem to be very vocal. Sometimes they're very well organized. Everyone is single-minded. Most university towns are rather stuffy. But Missoula has a very strong blue-collar element which makes it a REAL town instead of a university town." It is also, he believes, a wonderful town in which to raise a family.

He has so many good writers to choose from in publishing the Missoulian, he says, that making assignments can become a problem. "People live here by choice," he says. "It is as far from an apathetic community as you can get."

The Missoulian *built a new plant in 1985 just above the Clark Fork River at Higgins Avenue.*

6 THE UNIVERSITY

The University of Montana may be tied with the trucking industry for economic rank, but there is no contest as to which contributes more to Missoula's culture, lifestyle and all-around charm.

Dr. Donald Habbe, academic vice president of the university, is a political scientist and a native of Wisconsin. "Missoula seems to attract people who are interesting, active and on the move," he says. "It is heterogeneous and diverse. We love to argue and we almost tend to celebrate our discord. That's what makes it an interesting place to live."

The university's enrollment increased dramatically to a high of 11,000 students during the ten-year period from 1964 to 1974, but now stands at about 9,000. Faculty-student ratio is one to 19. UM has the state's largest international student enrollment, with many coming here from the Pacific Rim nations.

The Maureen and Mike Mansfield Foundation, which oversees the Mansfield Center on campus and an educational and cultural exchange program to be headquartered north of Missoula, on Flathead Lake, is a big draw for resident and nonresident students alike. Founded in honor of Montana's distinguished Mike Mansfield and his wife, Maureen, the foundation works to further Ambassador Mansfield's long-standing commitment to improving America's relations with its neighbors in the Pacific Rim.

On campus, the new five-story Mansfield Library is the sole repository of the former U.S. Senate majority leader's congressional papers; it also houses material from his ambassadorial assignment to

The Grizzly, sculptor Rudy Autio's version of the University of Montana's symbol.
Facing page: Main Hall, an administration building, characterizes the turn-of-the-century birth of the campus.

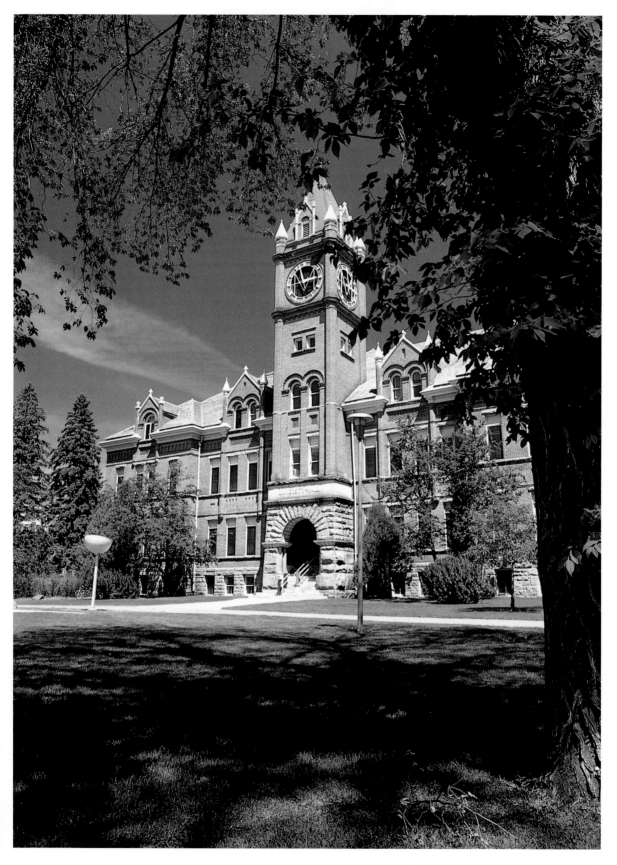

Japan. The history of the region is recorded here in the 6,000-volume Northwest Collection, with emphasis on the early fur trade, the Lewis & Clark Expedition, Montana Indians and Missoula history. The library also is headquarters for the Maureen and Mike Mansfield Center, which promotes programs for both undergraduate and graduate students preparing for careers in public life.

The composition of the university's student body has changed in recent years, with the influx of large numbers of "nontraditional" students—former college drop-outs who have returned, people working part-time, women planning to re-enter the job market after raising families. The average age of students is 25 or 26. Night school has been instituted to accommodate these students.

Apparently a university wasn't considered much of a plum back in the 1890s when the fight over the location of the state capital erupted. Anaconda, Helena, Boulder, Butte, Bozeman, Deer Lodge and Great Falls vied for the title of state capital. Missoula was the only town to bid for the university, which opened in a refurbished schoolhouse in 1895 with five university students and 45 "college preparatory" students.

The total budget for the first year of operation was $12,531.71. With its allotment of $1,575, the library bought 817 volumes and paid the $20-a-month salary of the librarian, who happened to be the president's daughter. The janitor received $60.

The proliferation of higher-education institutions in Montana in 1893 was set in motion by the first legislature, which passed an act founding four units of higher education: the College of Agriculture and Mechanic Arts in Bozeman, the State University in Missoula, the State Normal School (teachers' college) in Dillon,

and the School of Mines in Butte.

Northern Montana College in Havre was established in 1913; Eastern Montana College of Education in Billings, in 1925.

UM's first president, Dr. Oscar Craig, left the legacy of the University Oval, which was patterned after the campus of Purdue University, where he had taught history and political science before coming to Montana.

The university's second president, Dr. Clyde A. Duniway, was fired by the State Board of Education after four years, because his "administrative ideas did not agree with what the Board considers should be the policy of the State university." The Board chose to omit a paragraph from Dr. Duniway's final report, as "not pertinent to existing conditions nor conducive to the best interests of the institution." The paragraph concerned "the defects in the system of divided units and their government in Montana."

Thus began the game of musical chairs which has seen 16 presidents (plus six acting

presidents) come and go at the University of Montana in 91 years, for an average tenure of little more than five years. Montana State University at Bozeman has had only half as many. (Dr. James Koch, formerly of Ball State University, Indiana, became the university's 17th president in 1986.)

The Missoula campus has a statewide reputation for intellectual ferment and controversy. During the 1960s, UM became Montana headquarters for the student unrest that erupted across the nation in response to the war in Vietnam. The university's tradition of political activism has its roots in the activities and interests of its earliest faculty and students.

In 1919 Dr. Louis Levine of the Department of Economics and Sociology prepared a series of monographs on the subject of mine taxation. President Edward Sisson and Edward Elliott, chancellor of the University System, approved them for publication, although they were critical of state laws that permitted the mining industry to escape paying its

44

fair share of taxes. Fearing the documents might offend Montana's giant Anaconda copper mining company and lose the company's support for the university, Chancellor Elliott later reneged and suggested indefinite postponement. Levine published his findings at his own expense and was summarily suspended by Elliott.

The subsequent brouhaha had statewide repercussions. President Sisson supported Levine, and the student body protested his suspension. The *Butte Miner* editorialized: "The parents and guardians of this state have delegated supervisory control of the university to certain duly constituted authorities. The duty of these authorities is very plain... Students have nothing whatsoever to say about it." Neither, apparently, did the president.

Professor Levine was eventually reinstated with back pay, following an investigation by the American Association of University Professors.

When, in 1926, the phrase "son-of-a-bitch" appeared in *The Frontier,* the campus literary magazine, the state's major daily newspapers (owned by the Anaconda Company) demanded the resignation of H. G. Merriam, the magazine's sponsoring professor, and censure of the university on grounds of moral turpitude.

The appearance of Vardis Fisher's novel *Passions Spin the Plot,* on the leisure reading shelf of the university library in 1935, resulted in a ruling by the Board of Education that the novel and "all books of a similar character should be removed from the shelves of the libraries of all of the units of the University System." The action provoked a loud protest from librarian Phillip Keeney and H.G. Merriam, chairman of the English Department, as well as widespread criticism from students and from the academic community throughout the Northwest. Ultimately, the board moderated its stand and placed responsibility for "good taste" on all university officers and faculties.

At about the same time an article entitled "Hire Learning in Montana" appeared in *The Pacific Weekly,* criticizing the University for cancelling Eugene O'Neill's *Ah, Wilderness,* because the play included a scene with a prostitute.

Leslie Fiedler set the whole

Left: The University area is one of broad, shady avenues. Affluence may have moved to other parts of town but elegance remains.
Bottom: The campus seems like an extension of the river-front park system. This is in McCormick Park.

"What I had been expecting I do not clearly know: zest, I suppose, naivete, a ruddy and straightforward kind of vigor—perhaps even honest brutality. What I found seemed at first glance reticent, sullen, weary—full of self-sufficient stupidity; a little later it appeared simply inarticulate, with all the dumb pathos of what cannot declare itself… I felt a kind of innocence behind it, but an innocence difficult to distinguish from simple ignorance. In a way there was something heart-rending in dealing with people who had never seen, for instance, a Negro, or a Jew or a Servant, and were immune to all their bitter meanings; but the same people, I knew, had never seen an art museum or a ballet or even a movie in any language but their own, and the poverty of experience had left the possibilities of the human face in them incompletely realized."

To those angered by his essay, it didn't matter much that Fiedler, a popular teacher, set about remedying all the above in his fully-enrolled classes of the state's young.

state on its ear with his 1955 essay entitled "Montana: or the End of Jean-Jacques Rousseau," in which he described "the Montana face":

During the 1960s, the publication of four-letter words in the campus newspaper, *The Kaimin,* under the editorship of David Rorvik, received widespread publicity. Copies of the newspaper found their way to every legislative desk on the day the university's funding was up for vote.

Lt. Col. (ret.) Keith Angwin, head of the university's Reserve Officer Training Corps, led a drive to defeat a 6-mill University System levy in 1968, complaining to the State Board of Regents about "gutter language" and obscene material in University of Montana English classes, and "an instructor who seems to disregard good ethics and is continuously involved in activities detrimental to our society." The following October *The Kaimin* reported that Col. Angwin had "pleaded guilty in Salt Lake City to 'seeking sex acts for hire'."

The University of Montana has produced 23 Rhodes Scholars and such renowned graduates as Jeannette Rankin, nationally acclaimed jurist Judge William Jameson, maternal and child

health authority Dr. Jessie Bierman, physicist Harold Urey and Ambassador Mike Mansfield.

Harold G. Merriam, renaissance man, defender of academic freedom, Rhodes Scholar and professor from 1919 to retirement in 1954, wrote a history of the University of Montana in 1970. As founder and editor of *Frontier and Midland,* a literary magazine descended from *The Frontier,* Dr. Merriam launched such writers as A.B. Guthrie, Jr., Wallace Stegner, Grace Stone Coates, and Dorothy M. Johnson.

A granddaughter, Ginny Merriam, who summered at the Merriam cabin in Glacier National Park, tells of her grandparents arriving there with watermelons and wheels of cheese, to spend the days hiking and fishing in the mountains. Ginny, who came from Indiana to graduate (with highest honors) from the university's School of Journalism, is a free-lance writer in Missoula. She says she "simply can't imagine living anyplace else."

7 AUTHOR, AUTHOR

Bill Kittredge is heir apparent of H.G. Merriam at the University of Montana.

The door to Kittredge's apartment in an ancient brick building just off North Higgins Avenue is open. Except for framed Monte Dolack posters on the walls, a jammed bookcase and a coffee table with half a dozen books placed facedown to mark the reader's place, the room is uncluttered. Bill sits in an easy chair reading *The Real West Marginal Way,* an autobiography of Richard Hugo, edited by Lois and James Welch and Ripley Hugo. It is freshly published.

I explain my mission: Why is every third person I meet in Missoula a writer?

Bill chuckles from the depths of his considerable bulk and gives credit to everyone but himself. "It all goes back to H.G. Merriam. He established a tradition of writing excellence at the university and gave people a chance to publish with his literary magazine, *Frontier and Midland.* He encouraged all sorts of writers...."

The tradition was continued by Leslie Fiedler who, according to Kittredge, "taught people to read and to read well," and by the poet Richard Hugo, a protege of Theodore Roethke at the University of Washington. Hugo came to Montana at age 40 from a job with Boeing in Seattle, and wrote and taught in Missoula until his death in 1982.

The Master of Fine Arts in Writing program was established at the university in 1966. Kittredge came here to teach from the University of Iowa Writers' Workshop, after earning a degree in General

William Kittredge.

Annick Smith.

Agriculture at Oregon State University. He had grown up on a ranch in eastern Oregon, near Adel, where there was a sign, 'next gas station 86 miles' and it wasn't kidding.

"All sorts of people were attracted here by Dick Hugo," Kittredge continues. "They come and they stay." Off the top of his head he lists Montana writers—James Welch, Rick de Marinis, Earl Ganz, Bryan Di Salvatore, James Crumley, the late Kim Williams, Steve Krauzer, Bob Wrigley, Paul Zarzyski, Bill Finnegan, David Long, Ralph Beer, Leonard Robinson, Beth Ferris, Dan Whipple, Richard and Christina Ford. I had the impression that he could have listed many more. "Five books have been published this month from one block on Wylie Street in Missoula," says Kittredge.

As to why Missoula, Kittredge cites Thomas More's *Utopia,* where the ideal community size is similar to Missoula's 60,000 population. "There is lots of diversity here, lots of networking. It is a mixture of a small town and a city. I can't think of a better place to live. As for writers, there's no backbiting, no jealousy. We all help each other."

Kittredge currently is collaborating with the producer of the movie *Heartland,* Annick Smith, on a movie based on Norman Maclean's *A River Runs Through It.*

Smith is a stunning woman—even, or maybe especially, in blue jeans. Tall, with a mop of straight, gray hair piled on top of her head, she exudes life. Mother of four grown sons, she came to the university with her husband, from Chicago by way of the University of Washington, at the urging of their friend Richard Hugo. They were already hooked on filmmaking. Her husband died in 1974.

Why does she choose to live in Missoula? "The stuff going on here is first rate and the people are first rate."

Up past Greenough Park, along Rattlesnake Creek, in a pleasant Victorian house behind a picket fence on Wylie Street, we find James Welch. But not before we are greeted by an enthusiastic golden retriever who presents us with a slipper. Jim smiles a lot and his voice is soft. He is a gentle man.

Currently serving on the Montana Board of Pardons, he is "putting together" a novel based on the experience. Welch is of Gros Ventre-Blackfeet blood. While Indians comprise only 11 percent of Montana's population, they represent 24 percent of the prison population. Welch, who initially was reluctant to serve on the parole board, finds he is spending more and more time at the Swan River Youth Camp, a branch of the state prison. "There, but for the

grace of God, goes anybody," he says.

We are lucky to find him home as he has been touring the state promoting his latest novel, *Fools Crow*. His first, well received, novel, *Winter in the Blood,* has been re-issued by Penguin Books. It has become required reading for college courses on Native Americans. *Riding the Earthboy 40,* his book of poetry, is now out of print. In addition to writing, he is frequently a visiting professor of English and American Indian Studies at the University of Washington and at Cornell University.

Welch, who was born in Browning on the Blackfeet Indian Reservation, also has lived in South Dakota and in Minneapolis. He studied at Northern Montana College

and the University of Minnesota before coming to the University of Montana for the MFA in Writing program. Although he had begun to write before coming to Missoula, he says: "I learned so much about writing from Hugo and Kittredge. They can teach you the mechanics, how to use the language effectively, how to create the sense of tension necessary to any book. Those are the things that a young writer needs help with—the tricks of the trade."

He credits his wife, Lois, a professor of English at the university, with helping him in his career. The two have lived in Greece and Mexico and have travelled extensively in Europe. Welch gets to Browning every year and remains in close touch with his family. But Missoula is home.

James Welch.

Bryan Di Salvatore was doing the final editing on a full-length feature on dynamite (of all things) for *The New Yorker* when we met for lunch. The handsome, black-moustached native of California came to the University's MFA in Writing program from Yale, where Richard Hugo had taught briefly.

Di Salvatore's explanation of Missoula's profusion of writers comes from his friend, author James Crumley *(The Wrong Case, The Last Good Kid, Dancing Bear):* "Missoula used to be at the bottom of a lake. Writers like damp, sticky places."

He himself sizes Missoula up as "a really schizo town in the best sense of the word. There's so much talent here that it's a little Athens, a little Paris. It's okay to be a bohemian in Missoula. University towns tend to be 'genteel,' but not Missoula. People do outdoor things here, but never in a formalized way. Their canoes or skis are affixed to their cars. After a day's work, they take off into the mountains to go camping."

Or they can compete in "The Festival of Champions," a two-day, four-event extravaganza created by Missoula's writing crowd in 1985. The festival has included a two-hour competition with the grandiose

Left: West of Lolo.
Facing page: Dawn from Blue Mountain Lookout.

title "Trash Fishing in America." It was held on the Clark Fork River between the Van Buren and Madison Street bridges within the city limits. Invitations read: "Any twit with a $400 Orvis rod and an Ernie Schwiebert streamer can catch trout, but not everyone has what it takes to wade into a radioactive slough" after carp, squawfish and suckers. The winning catch—a 13-ounce squawfish. Trout, if caught, had to be thrown back.

Grand prize for the festival was a two-foot bronzed figurine of a briefcase-carrying yuppie, together with a bonus prize of a pair of Barrel Rock chickens, alive.

The 1986 "Festival of Champions" featured "Road Kill," with the prize a paté-and-bread replica of a dead snake embossed with tire tracks, a dish enjoyed by all.

Other delights of the city, according to Di Salvatore, are the record store Rockin' Rudy's—a store "better than any town deserves." And book stores—The University Book Store, Fact and Fiction, Freddy's Feed and Read, and Little Professor. Then there's

Bill Vaughn's graphics shop, where you can buy a T-shirt picturing a duck with the legend "Missoula, Montana—a place…sort of." Uniquely beautiful posters by Missoula artist Monte Dolack can be found at his studio above the Top Hat bar.

Says Di Salvatore, "The purpose of an education is to develop a sense of irony." It's an appropriate observation. In his mid-30s, Bryan Di Salvatore is just achieving recognition. In the meantime, he has enjoyed every minute of his time in Missoula, Montana. It's impossible to estimate how much money Missoula's "sweat shop" writers contribute to the economy. Laboring away at their individual typewriters and word processors in their secluded cabins, attics, basements and offices, many of them manage to make a living. Some do much better. Writing could hardly be classified as a secondary industry. But it is definitely a homegrown industry and its practitioners might better be labeled entrepreneurs.

8 DOERS

Dan Lambros, of Lambros Realty, exudes enthusiasm—about his brainchild, Southgate Mall, about his Village Motor Inn, about the housing developments that creep into every valley. In Missoula Lambros Realty has a finger in every pie. As to the charge that "The Mall" destroyed Higgins Avenue, he says: "We're proud of Southgate Mall, of its design and landscaping and what goes on there. We wanted something good for Missoula. As for the downtown, it is being revitalized. Actually, we enhanced it."

As to why people choose to live in Missoula, he says, "People vote with their feet. When you add up our assets—the university, the public school system, the recreation facilities of the area (lakes, streams, hunting, fishing)—you find that our greatest asset is the quality of the people who live here. And why are they here? Because they want to be, not because they have to be. Most of them could probably make more money someplace else."

Dan Lambros talks with pride of his immigrant father, Peter Lambros, who left his native village of Paleohorian, Greece when he was 14 and came to Butte, where he had a cousin. His first job was selling popcorn in Columbia Gardens. His first business was a candy store. When he was 40, he returned to Greece where he met and married his wife. The couple moved to Missoula in 1929 and became the parents of Dan, George and Helen. The story is that the Lambros Real Estate Agency began when

Symbol of growth, modernity and the growing south side of town, Southgate Mall.

Peter Lambros presented each of his children with a piece of run-down property and the option to dispose of it.

Dan philosophizes, "As we move from an industrial society into an information society, I think we have all the ingredients in place to make Missoula very attractive to such industries as bio-tech, high-tech—quality endeavors which will be attracted here because of our lifestyle. We're talking about brainpower. In business the most important thing is your work force. We have got to tell potential industries that their people will be happy here. We don't want the kind of people or industries which will degrade our way of life. I think we are putting in place all the ingredients to make this happen. We are going to live by our own design. We are not going to be victims. We have got to figure out who we want—and those people who are going to destroy what we have here, we don't want. We must take control of our own lives.

"In the industrial age, transportation and location were all-important," he adds. "In the information age, all you need is the technology and equipment. With Mountain Bell Telephone we have state-of-the-art technology at our fingertips. We can be automatically piped into the system."

An ardent supporter of the University of Montana from which he holds both business and law degrees, Dan is equally devoted to the city of Missoula, which has been good to him and his family. The three Lambros daughters, Maria, Meliora and Demetria, are his special pride. Meliora is currently playing viola with a trio touring the east coast.

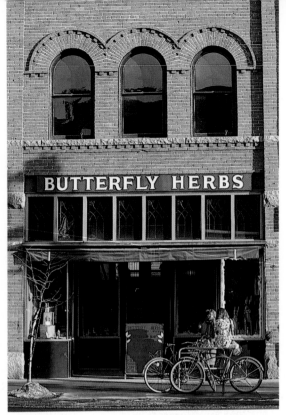

Downtown promotes the personal touch of "main-street" shopping and its distinctive businesses. Scott Sproull is president of the Downtown Association.

Scott Sproull was on the telephone discussing plans for putting up all-white Christmas lights in downtown Missoula. Scott runs the Hide and Sole Leather Shop and is president of the Missoula Downtown Association, which has 800 individual members, 600 of them downtown business-people. In addition to Christmas lighting, the association plants and maintains the wrought-iron baskets that hang from downtown light-poles. Hand-wrought by metal sculptor Russell Smith, Jr., the flower-filled baskets have been such a success that they have had to be raised to be kept from the reach of passers-by.

The Missoula Downtown Association has launched a campaign to lure customers away from shopping centers with billboards asking, "Tired of being malled?" Says Sproull, "You can't be at an interior mall at the Christmas season without feeling like a lemming." The campaign isn't liable to win many friends at Southgate Mall.

Scott Sproull followed Lewis and Clark to Missoula. A Michigan native, he needed more information for a paper he was writing on the Lewis and Clark Expedition for a class at Western Illinois University. Having $200 in capital, he spent $100 for a used car and headed west. He ran out of gas in Missoula, where he found everything he needed to know about Lewis and Clark at the University of Montana library. He submitted the paper by mail, got an A on it, and never went back to Michigan or Illinois.

He explains, "I canoe a lot. Out here it is totally different. Your peer group wants to get out and do things. But I couldn't find a job. I was working for the sewer treatment

plant, which paid me $150 a week to sleep and answer the phone, and taking classes at the university. Some friends of mine had started a leather business in Illinois and weren't doing well. I bought the business in July of 1975 and moved it to Missoula."

Now Sproull is married and

the father of four children. "The advantages of raising kids here are overwhelming," he says. "We take them hiking at least once a week. My wife runs five miles a day."

Looking younger than his 52 years, and hardly like a captain of industry, Dennis R. Washington greets visitors in

an elegantly appointed corner office of Washington Corporation's new Missoula headquarters on Reserve Street. Seeing him surrounded by art objects, oriental rugs, a Chinese lacquer screen and a scale model of his yacht, *HMS Lark,* it is hard to imagine that this Missoula native son lived with his grandmother in a section house on the Milwaukee railroad right-of-way when he went to Missoula County High School.

Owner not only of Washington Corporation, but also of Modern Machinery (operating in Washington, Arizona,

Above: The Glacier Building at the heart of downtown, once the Florence Hotel, doubtless Missoula's classiest in its day.
Left: The store is The Bon, but to many Missoulians the building always will be The Mercantile. Note the Russell Smith handwrought flower basket.

Montana and Wyoming); Equipco Inc. (a repair subsidiary), Western Transport Crane and Rigging (trucking), and Industrial Constructors, all headquartered in Missoula, the straightforward "Denny" Washington, son of a construction worker, says with no apologies, "Listen, I learned this business laying on my ass on the ground underneath machinery."

That began when he was 15 and worked during the summer as an equipment oiler on the construction of Ross Dam in Bellingham, Washington. Later he worked for his uncle, Bud King, a Missoula contractor, progressing from foreman to project superintendent and finally vice president of King-McLaughlin

Construction Company. In 1964 he formed Washington Construction Co. with a $30,000 loan from Gary Gallagher of Missoula and a used tractor he bought with no down payment. His first job was building the parking lot of the Visitors' Center on Going-to-the-Sun Highway in Glacier National Park. Jobs for the Park Service and highway department followed. His most recent highway job was a $16.3 million section of the interstate north of Butte.

In 1985 he bought the former Anaconda Mineral Company's Butte properties and is now shipping concentrated copper and molybdenum ore to Japan, Korea and England.

"Basically, we work west of the Mississippi," he says. In

addition to highway construction, open-pit mining and dams, the business has diversified into sales, rentals and transport of heavy equipment. Washington's corporations employ some 1,200 people, 130 of them in Missoula. "Whether it's a dam or a mine or a highway, we'll do it as long as it's tough, big work."

When he was eight, Dennis Washington was one of the last pre–Salk-vaccine victims of poliomyelitis. You would never know it to look at his 6'2" frame, but he says it still interferes with his tennis game.

His friend, lawyer Milt Datsopoulos, introduced Dennis to Phyllis Peterson, a Paxson school teacher and former University of Montana homecoming queen. They were married in 1964. She operates "P.J.'s," an interior design shop on Broadway, and was responsible for the decoration of the Washington Corporation offices. They have two teenaged sons.
The Washingtons recently built a home in the Rattlesnake—with a tennis court.

"Why do I want to live in

Missoula?" Washington asks. "Well, I could live anywhere in the West. Missoula is the best place that I know of to raise kids and I love it. I'm a Montana boy and proud of it. The people here are stable and they work a little harder, plus we don't have a bunch of flakes. It's a little more relaxed and a lot less competitive than California, where they think we're a bunch of hicks. Okay, then, so I'm a hick. At least here you don't get carried away with yourself and you don't get to thinking you're a big deal."

Asked about his $1 million gift to the University of Montana for its new Washington-Grizzly stadium, he says simply, "Montana doesn't have to be second class."

Walking through the complex of buildings which house his various enterprises, we paused before a monumental "580" loader. One tire on the machine costs $26,000!

Bill Potts, a long-time member of the Missoula City Council and office manager of Local 885 of the United Paper Workers Union, lives in a small cottage in Orchard Homes. A vegetable garden,

raspberry bushes and straw-berry plants and fruit trees grow in the fenced yard and evidence of the fall harvest is gathered in the kitchen. Reading materials are ev-erywhere. The 70-year-old Bill—a small, friendly man with very blue eyes—wages a battle to keep his reluctant pipe lit and to keep his devoted old dog sufficiently petted as we talk. Although his appearance and manner belie it, Bill has influence in Missoula.

Near the Missoula White Pine and Sash mill on the north side. Despite its university airs, Missoula has been largely a working-class town. At lower right is one of the infamous teepee burners once common to lumber mills through-out the region.

Bill is head of Missoula's most stable and well-paid work force, a union of about 600, of which 175 to 200 are salaried workers, and keeps in touch with the labor situation in Missoula. And he is worried. The wage "give-backs" of the men working for Champion International at Bonner resulted, he said, when the company threatened to close the plant and run it with management people. This "give-back" amounting to $3,600

apiece per year, for a thousand men, during the two-year period of the contract, will put pressure on the upcoming contract for wages and benefits of the paper workers.

"Anybody who doesn't wear rose-colored glasses knows it is going to be tough next sum-mer," says Bill. "They are going to throw the book at us. Our union voted to raise our dues by $10 a month and send those dues to the mills that are on strike. That may be a way

for labor to fight back at these plant closures and give-backs. All the lumber workers in the northwest are nervous for fear that if they go on strike, the companies will bring in management and strike-breakers from the midwest. Our only hope is not to take the men on strike until the economy rebounds."

Bill's concern is not just lo-cal, but national. "The thing that bothers me is that there are going to be only the real rich and the poor in this country. We are decimating the middle-income people. If we get rid of that middle sector our government is not going to be stable. The service trades have been expanding, but we need smokestack industries and agriculture. The outlook is dim for people in service industries and labor and the business outlook is not good for Missoula. People are not buying big-ticket items. Business notices it when a thousand men lose $3,600 out of their pay for two years."

Bill Potts has lived in Mis-soula since 1949. Born in the Blackfoot Valley, he has worked in the woods, worked as a heavy equipment opera-tor on Cabinet Gorge and Noxon dams, operated a crane for American Crystal Sugar and even worked for two years as a heavy equip-ment mechanic at Thule Air Force Base 700 miles south of the North Pole. Both Bill and his wife Marian, a retired school teacher, like to hunt and fish as do most of the people they know. "A good share of them own four-wheel-drive vehicles and boats," he says. "Working people love this country."

The Federal Building (top). Regional offices of the U.S. Forest Service and other government agencies have a major economic impact, as does the Burlington Northern Railroad (left).

9 HOSPITAL WARS

In 1872, Washington J. McCormick, Missoula's first attorney, sold three blocks of land and a house for $1,500 to the fathers of St. Ignatius Mission on the condition that they establish a hospital in Missoula. Even in those days it was a bargain, although it turned out that the "house" had most recently seen service as a chicken coop. It was up to the nuns of the Montreal order of Sisters of Providence to make it into a hospital.

On April 19, 1873, Mother Caron, Sister Mary Victor and Sister Mary Edward, accompanied by Father Palladino, rode horseback the 28 miles from St. Ignatius to Missoula and set to work. They began by hauling water from a nearby stream and using plenty of soap and carbolic acid, the leading disinfectant of the day. Mattresses were made by stuffing straw into ticking. When St. Patrick Hospital opened four months later, the sisters provided compassionate care, cleanliness and hope. Their only medical equipment consisted of stethoscopes and hypodermic syringes.

In the first hospital register, dated August 1873 to July 1905, the sisters documented cases of measles, scarlet fever,

Washington J. McCormick, Sr.
MANSFIELD LIBRARY, UNIV. OF MONTANA

Below: St. Patrick's Hospital, no date. One of its first patients was Father Ravalli, famous for his missionary work at St. Mary Mission, founded in 1852 at Stevensville, shown at left. PHOTOS COURTESY OF LEN ECKEL
Right: St. Patrick's today.

smallpox, malaria, St. Vitus dance, St. Anthony's fire, piles, influenza, bilious fever, neuralgia, hypochondria, whooping cough, insanity, heat stroke, Rocky Mountain spotted fever, dysentery, "LaGrippe," pneumonia, diphtheria and snakebite. There were also broken bones, stabbings, gunshot wounds, accidents of all kinds, and frozen feet and hands in winter. Women were rarely hospitalized, except for the "confinement" of childbirth. Alcoholism, or "the liquor habit" as the nuns delicately called it, then as now, took its toll.

The small building with its crude furnishings served as hospital, chapel and living quarters until a 32-foot addition was built in 1882. In 1885 a three-story building with beds for 90 patients was built.

The second recorded patient at St. Patrick's was "Reverend

Father Anthony Ravalli, Italian, age 64, Jesuit father." Father Ravalli, for whom the town and county were named, had come to St. Mary's mission near Stevensville, bringing

skills in architecture, carpentry, woodcarving and medicine. Quite understandably, he was admitted to the hospital for treatment of "general debility," or exhaustion.

The Sisters of Providence, whose original designation was Sisters of Charity, Servants of the Poor, charged no fees, but accepted donations from patients. A contract for care of the county's sick and insane paid $10 for a medical case and $18 for a mental case. Although the St. Ignatius mission provided the sisters with a small income, it was inadequate. To get money for furniture, supplies and additional space, the sisters depended on "begging trips" to nearby farms and mining camps, and the generosity of citizens.

A new St. Patrick Hospital annex with 217 beds was completed in 1984 at a cost of $37.4 million. Every patient has a room with a view and the design allows nurses to reach any patient in fewer than 30 steps. The hospital offers open-heart surgery and a cardiac catheterization laboratory, and houses the Western Montana Region Cancer Center. It has helicopter ambulance service and a chemical dependency program. Employing 750 people, including about 200

Missoula Community Med-
ical Center, a 115-bed hospital,
is the state's 19th-largest private employer, with 714 employees and a $23.6 million
budget. Until recently it provided most of the city's obstet-
rics services, and it features
the largest and most compre-
hensive rehabilitation program in the state, offering oc-
cupational, physical, and
speech and audiology therapy.

The 57-bed Missoula Gen-
eral Hospital, a former railroad hospital, has a new $11
million building. It features
emergency service and a
Short Stay Surgery Program,
as well as optometric services
and psychological counseling
and education services.

Out-patient treatment in
Missoula is offered by several

physicians, it is the 15th-
largest private employer in
the state. Regularly some 170
volunteers help out.

Today, three hospitals with a
total of 389 licensed beds, four
private long-term care facilities with a total of 338 beds, two
major clinics, and more than
1,300 medical personnel minister to the Missoula area's
health-care needs. There is
one physician for every 400
people, compared with a nationwide average of one physician per 1,000 people. It is said
that Missoula has more doc-
tors per capita than any other
city in the United States except
Boston.

Health care is big business
in Missoula. The health-care

industry employs nearly 2,500
and serves a large geographic
region, including the entire
western part of Montana and
sections of Idaho, with a
population of approximately
300,000. Altogether it is estimated that health-care workers received $41.9 million in
wages in 1984.

physician groups, including Western Montana Clinic, the city's largest and oldest, which recorded 97,000 patient visits in 1985. Begun by five physicians, it now has nearly 50 practicing in 14 different medical specialties. Another major clinic is the Blue Mountain Women's Clinic, which offers low-cost care for low-risk patients.

Unquestionably Missoula has optimum medical facilities. Might it even have too many? The *Missoulian* of October 7, 1986, editorialized:

"MISSOULA'S HEALTH-CARE SYSTEM: RX FOR DISASTER

"Missoula, a community of roughly 77,000, seems hardly capable of supporting three new and relatively new hospitals. Judging from the growing intensity of their competition, managers of the hospitals may have come to the same conclusion....

"The only hope for avoiding a hospital shakeout—and ultimately higher health-care costs—lies with the willingness of the three hospitals to cooperate and perhaps negotiate the delivery of health services. Perhaps there is an agency or organization willing to mediate talks among the hospital managers....Reasoned coordination of services won't completely fix this system gone amok. But the alternative—a ruinous hospital war—is worse."

Additional health-related services available in the Garden City range from Planned Parenthood and Birthright to Hospice. Those in distress can call the Crisis Center. Therapy is offered at the Mental Health Center, the University Clinical Psychology Center, the County Health Department and the Missoula Indian Alcohol and Drug Service.

Residents with a variety of problems can locate support groups: dealing with alcoholism, arthritis, bereavement, cancer, drugs, gambling, overeating; for nursing mothers, laryngectomees, parents, rape victims, singles, smokers, widows, women in transition, young parents.

Missoula is the place to receive help for many types of physical or psychological problems.

10 AMENITIES

I n 1860 the brothers James and Granville Stuart, mining and farming on Gold Creek, learned from passing Indians that there was a trunk of books in the Bitterroot Valley. They saddled their horses, rode the 150 miles and managed to buy five books, at $5.00 apiece, to read during the winter of 1860-1861. The books: illustrated editions of Shakespeare and Lord Byron, Headley's *Napoleon and His Marshals,* the Bible in French, and Adam Smith's *The Wealth of Nations.* Reading and "book learning" were established early as important, and even necessary, in Montana.

Historical museum at Fort Missoula

Missoula's first library collection began in 1875 when four men contributed $100 each to buy books. After that a "ladies circle" took over. The Missoula Public Library, consisting of two rented rooms and 519 books, was established in 1894. It wasn't until 1902 that a Carnegie grant of $12,500 made possible the first library building. The present handsome library at 301 East Main Street houses some 130,000 volumes and provides bookmobile services to Frenchtown, Nine Mile, Potomac, Greenough, Clearwater Junction, Seeley Lake, Clinton and Bonner.

Missoula has always felt an obligation to educate its young. In 1960 when Seeley Lake, a logging community 60 miles from Missoula but part of the Missoula County high school district, failed to produce a single high school graduate, it was determined that the longest school bus ride in the United States was a failure. The grueling ride, anxiety about road and weather conditions, lack of "social" contacts and participation in after-school functions, plus inability to get outside help from teachers or to use reference materials far outweighed the advantages of attending a large high school. One mother said, "You could see the weariness building up. My girl had to get up at five in the morning and she never got to bed before 11. She had such a cross disposition it made everybody in the family miserable."

Since there was not enough taxable valuation in the Seeley Lake area to build or support a high school, the Missoula County high school board voted to establish a "satellite" high school to be financed by a special levy on the whole high school district, particularly the town of Missoula. The measure carried handily, and the school was built. It may be the only high school in the country that has a fishing stream running through its grounds.

Now Missoula County high school district has an enroll-ment of 3,713 and 370 teachers in its four high schools. Loyola Sacred Heart and Valley Christian School provide private education with a religious orientation. Missoula School District One includes 16 elementary schools with more than 5,000 students and 370 teachers. The public school systems have long been noted for the excellence of their academic, athletic and artistic programs.

The Missoula Vocational-Technical Center adjacent to Sentinel High School is administered by the county high school board and offers 23 ca-

reer choices in such areas as heavy equipment operation, small engine repair, welding, business skills, computer science, licensed practical nursing, respiratory therapy, forestry and food preparation. There are currently 620 students enrolled. The Missoula facility is one of five such centers in the state.

Between the public school system and the university, there is no excuse for ignorance or lack of cultural awareness in Missoula.

The University of Montana inaugurated its performing arts center in 1985 with an original musical, *Cowboy.* Based on the life of Charles M. Russell and enlisting all the artistic efforts of the university, the production was smashing from its stage sets to its choreography. Missoula also has been treated with Menotti's Christmas opera, *Amahl and the Night Visitors,* a cooperative effort by Missoula Children's Theater, Missoula Symphony Orchestra, University of Montana and Front Street Dance Center.

Missoula has furnished its share of stars to the arts, including Judith Blegen, soprano with New York's Metropolitan Opera Company, Michael Smuin, choreographer and director of the San Francisco Ballet, and actor Carroll O'Connor.

Live theater, classic and foreign movies and an assortment of nightclubs featuring musical groups with such diverse titles as "Lost Creek Creek," "Sugarfoot," "Big Sky Mudflaps," "Zeros and Ones," "Western Draw," "Star Train," "Nasty

Habit" and "Motion" make it appear that an evening in front of the TV—two local stations, in addition to cable service—might be a rarity.

There are also 164 clubs and 12 fraternal organizations. Missoulians of various religious persuasion can find a home in one of the city's 74 churches.

Furthermore, it is possible to get to all these places for a mere 25 cents on the Mountain Line—with a cleverly drawn Mountain Lion on the side of each and every bus. Missoula's elderly ride for a dime.

The Missoula Senior Citizens' Center at 705 South Higgins has a membership of 2,200. Dues are $5 a year. It publishes a newspaper, *Blazing New Trails,* and sponsors almost any activity you can name—from shuffleboard to chartered tours. Coffee is 10 cents a cup. Meals, priced from $2 to $3 (the latter for Sundays and Thanksgiving), are served daily, and are supplemented by pancake suppers and potluck dinners. There's probably more dancing done at the Senior Center than anywhere else in Missoula, including the university—a dance every Friday night to live music and square dancing every Monday night (refreshments at intermission), cost: $2.25. Aerobics classes meet twice a week with a certified instructor. Canasta, bridge and pinochle can be played formally on Monday, Wednesday and Saturday, but informal sessions of cribbage and pitch go on non-stop.

Need a ride? Call the Senior Citizens mini-bus service. Specialized transportation is available for those not able to ride the bus. Services such as Meals on Wheels and in-home health support help the housebound. A service called "Elder Phone" enables seniors to get almost any information they need by making a single phone call.

Missoula's active branches of the Montana Senior Citizens Association, American Association of Retired Persons and the Gray Panthers, as well as Missoula Aging Services, assure political clout for seniors. The aged are offered many services in Missoula.

11 LIBERAL ARTS

T he University of Montana public radio station KUFM covers western Montana like the stars. It started small in 1965 as a training facility, an adjunct to the university's radio/television communications curriculum. It began its public service programming in 1973 and in 1974 joined National Public Radio. Today it ranks 10th among 300 public radio stations in the national network in per capita support. Last year its listeners contributed $130,000 in a seven-day fund-raising campaign.

Jyl Hoyt, the personality behind award-winning radio program, "Reflections in Montana."

KUFM broadcasts to Helena and Butte through translator stations and has a satellite station, KGPR, in Great Falls. It even has one devoted listener in Salmon, Idaho, who gets the station from a "freak bounce" off the surrounding mountains. About half of Montana, including such towns as Conrad and Big Sandy and Darby, can listen to special-interest programming, in-depth news, analysis and commentary on "Morning Edition" and "All Things Considered," and tune in on both classical music and high-class jazz. Children are treated daily to Marcia Dunn's hour-long program, "The Pea Green Boat."

Terry Conrad, KUFM's genial, bearded program director, came here in 1972 from Chicago. He says, "Looking back, it's amazing to me how tremendously we have grown and how strongly we are supported."

While federal appropriations for public broadcasting have been reduced in recent years, its listenership has been growing much faster than commercial broadcasting. Conrad acknowledges the difficulties

National Public Radio reaches western Montana through KUFM, which ranks tenth nationally in per-capita public support. KUFM's director, Terry Conrad.

and time involved in fund-raising, but points out that "contributing gives our listeners a stake in the well-being of the station. It gives them almost an emotional attachment."

A trained musician from the Sherwood School of Music and the University of Chicago, Conrad taught public school music and volunteered as a disk jockey at a jazz radio station before becoming hooked on public radio.

When he came to Missoula, "the station was off the air. My first job was to help four other people in moving the transmitter—I mean physically—to the top of 8,000-foot Big Sky Mountain 11 miles north of Snow Bowl," Conrad says. "It's been a wonderful experience for me to see how KUFM has taken on a life of its own. The calibre of people we are able to draw on for broadcasting is incredibly high."

Terry Conrad and his wife, Germaine, a German teacher, didn't come here for money. They wanted interesting work to do and wanted to raise their two children in the west. Missoula was the answer.

Jyl Hoyt's weekly 30-minute radio program "Reflections in Montana," tells Montanans about Montana. It airs not only on KUFM and KGPR but on a total of 25 stations in Montana, North Dakota and Washington. It is funded by a grant from the Montana Committee for the Humanities, as well as by other grants.

A native of Wyoming and a Peace Corps returnee who served two tours (one each in Guatemala and Liberia), Hoyt has created a program that has received the Amos Tuck Award from the School of Business at Dartmouth College "for outstanding reporting which improves the public's understanding of business and economic issues."

Jyl Hoyt says of herself, "I am a great listener. I listen to what people have to say. I go beyond news—I do analysis. The title of my program is 'Reflections' and I am trying to get people to stop and reflect on how the wheat we grow, the gold we mine, fits into a global picture. I try to give meaning to social movements in the state. People here relate to the land and a lot of our activities are molded by our relationship to the land."

Northern Lights Institute began in 1981 with a National Science Foundation planning grant. It is a research and education center serving Idaho, Montana and Wyoming. Its purpose is to examine major issues that affect the region's environment, economy and culture.

Funded mostly by private foundations, the organization is committed to environmental quality, economic diversity and the involvement of citizens in making decisions about their future. It publishes the bimonthly *Northern Lights Magazine.* It is also sponsoring "Visions of the Northern

West," an eight-part video series documenting the history and heritage of this region, as part of the 1989 and 1990 centennials of North and South Dakota, Montana, Wyoming, Idaho and Washington. Annick Smith *(Heartland)* and Anne Stadler (KING-TV) are co-producers of the series.

The Native Home of Hope, a collection of two dozen essays describing life, hope, fear and the future of Idaho, Montana and Wyoming, was published by the institute in 1986.

The Montana Committee for the Humanities is headquartered in Missoula. It sponsored more than 30 forums, workshops, exhibits, seminars, exhibits, and radio programs during 1986.

Missoula is Montana's Hollywood. Beth Ferris based her screenplay for *Heartland* on Elinore Stewart's *Letters of a Woman Homesteader.* The critically acclaimed film touched the heart of all descendants of western homesteaders and has been widely shown both in theaters and on television. Most recently she has co-produced *Contrary Warriors,* a documentary on

Lower Miller Creek.

the Crow tribe. Earlier she had worked on short educational films such as *Wildflowers of Montana* and *Year of the Mountain Goats,* and a documentary, *Next Year Country,* on the social impacts of energy development in Idaho, Washington, Montana and North Dakota.

And then there's music. The 90-member Missoula Symphony Orchestra is in its 35th year. Conductor Joseph Henry, associate professor of music at the University, is a composer as well as conductor. He holds three degrees from Eastman School of Music in New York. Symphony members include musicians of all stripes and professional background. Some are graduates of the Missoula County High School Youth Symphony, having taken up an instrument under the direction of its long-time conductor, Harold Herbig, who also studied at Eastman. Others are musicians of near-professional calibre with extensive training.

Backed by the Women's Association of the Symphony, and sometimes joined by the Symphony Chorale under the

direction of Joseph Mussulman
and guest artists of national
renown, the orchestra plays
five formal concerts each year
plus a springtime "pops" con-
cert—all memorable Missoula
evenings.

Whatever musical talent a
person has, there's an outlet.
Men of all ages can join the
Missoula Mendelssohn Club,
which recently toured Europe.
Women who want to sing four-
part harmony can join the
Sweet Adelines, who perform
25 to 30 times a year. Male
barbershoppers can join the
Rocky Mountainaires.

The Missoula City Band
performs free concerts at Bonner Park each Wednesday
evening during the summer.
Parents take their children,
grandmothers their knitting,
to enjoy the work of band-
leader Alex Stepanzoff, who
came to Missoula from Russia
as the University of Montana's
first foreign exchange student.
Stepanzoff is known as the
Arthur Fiedler of Missoula.

The Missoula Blues and Jazz
Society invites enthusiasts of
these persuasions.

Rudy Autio, whose studio is
on Duncan Street up the Rat-

tlesnake, is shaped somewhat
like one of the hand-built
vessels for which he is famous.
A Finn who grew up in Butte,
he studied art at Montana
State College (now Montana
State University), then went to
teach and work at the Archie
Bray Foundation in Helena,
and later at the University of
Montana. Now retired from the
university, he devotes full time
to his art.

Autio can no longer be called
a potter. He says his vessels
are "containers, not pots," but
that they are not meant to hold

anything. "To put a feather in
them would violate the inten-
tion of what they are about."

Autio is a sculptor and painter of clay. His convoluted con-
structions are etched, then painted, with sensuous figures of
women and horses following
the planes and undulations of
the vessels. Colored clay and
glazes and innumerable fir-
ings are involved in the production.

Surrounded by some two
dozen of his art objects, which
sell for $5,000 to $15,000 each,
Autio says that this period is

the very best of all his professional life. He and his wife, Lela, herself a painter and fabric art designer, travel widely. In his ancestral Finland, where he refreshed his knowledge of the Finnish language, he made contact with the weavers who produced the grand tapestry he designed for the foyer of the university's performing arts center.

The internationally known Autio rates the work of area artists as outstanding. "Artists come here because the world is shrinking and it is becoming more and more difficult to live and work in a place like New York City."

The Missoula Museum of the Arts, housed in the former Missoula Public Library, mounts some 15 exhibitions of regional, national and international art each year, and promotes art appreciation through gallery talks, films and family events. Mary Cummings is curator. Twelve private and university-affiliated galleries, with such intriguing names as "Marie's ART-eries" and "Artful Nuance," display and sell student and professional artists' work.

The arts, all of them, burgeon in Missoula. Missoula is probably the only town in Montana to put a piece of public art at the end of Main Street, a red metal sculpture called "Crossings," by artist Taag Peterson. It was financed by the Missoula Redevelopment Agency and the sale of centennial coins, and sponsored by the Missoula Public Art Committee. Harold Balaz, a Spokane artist, was called in as interpreter/explainer of the

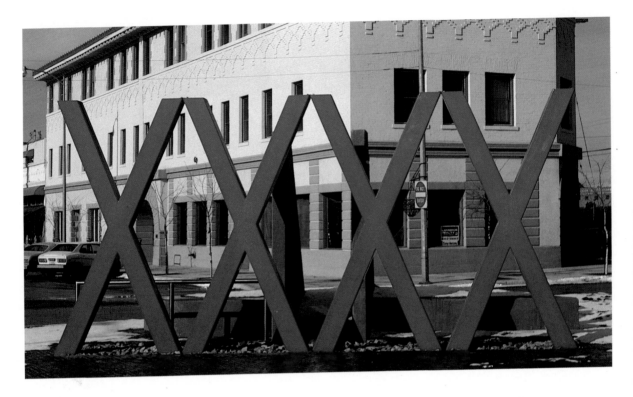

piece. Of it, he said: "Public art shows that we care enough to make this corner of the world a more beautiful place. That's what's important…It's impossible to please everybody with a piece of public art. If the art did please everybody, chances are it would be boring."

Marilyn Bruya, of the University of Montana art department, pointed out that the purpose of art is "to pose questions, not to give answers." Dana Boussard, a member of the Missoula Public Art Committee, said that the purpose of "Crossings" is not to be pretty, but to provoke a response. It did.

As the controversy rages, "Crossings," said to evoke images of a railroad, stands beside the retired locomotive that long ago pulled trains into the Northern Pacific depot at the end of Higgins Avenue. One commentator said the sculpture looked like an x'd out typographical error.

Returning to the first chapter of this book: "Missoula is addictive. It inspires a peculiar possessiveness in those who live here." Whether our possessiveness shows in wrangling over public sculpture or in dozens of other civic projects, so many of us do indeed love Missoula.

Facing page: "Crossings" metal sculpture at the end of North Higgins Avenue. As with most acts of public life in cerebral Missoula it provoked myriad responses.

12 GEOLOGY

**by Dave Alt,
Professor of Geology,
University of Montana**

Before we get to the Missoula Valley, it might be good to stop for a moment to look at the rocks in the mountains. Except for the Bitterroot Range, all the mountains around the Missoula Valley consist of an assortment of very hard sedimentary rocks, mostly mudstones and sandstones. All those rocks were laid down as sediments during Precambrian time, probably between 1,000 and 1,500 million years ago. That is impressive antiquity, even by the wildly extravagant age standards of geology.

You can see those rocks almost anywhere around the Missoula Valley, or, throughout much of western Montana. A walk along the old railroad bed through Hellgate Canyon provides an excellent view, as does a hike in the Rattlesnake or on Blue Mountain. Any pile of pebbles in the Missoula Valley furnishes hundreds of nice glimpses of a variety of Precambrian sedimentary rocks.

No animals lived on the earth when those rocks formed—only the most primitive kinds of green plants, just scummy growths of blue-green algae. A few minutes spent sorting through here will show you evidence of the absence of animals. Look for rocks full of very thin sedimentary layers, color bands a fraction of an inch thick. Those very fine sedimentary details are common in Precambrian rocks, rather rare in younger rocks laid down since animals began to dig and crawl in freshly deposited mud and sand.

Fossil blue-green algae are much harder to find. The easiest kind to spot, called stromatolites, are too big to show up well in pebbles. They look almost like clusters of Brussels sprouts embedded in the rocks; in fact, they are little algal

Top: Finely layered Precambrian mudstone laid down more than a billion years ago, before any animals lived on earth. This and similar rock formations are the bedrock all around the Missoula Valley. DAVE ALT
Facing page: Hot springs like Lolo's once-popular commercial development are vents from the vast reservoir of hot or molten rock at depth.

LOLO HOT SPRINGS

THE TRAVELERS PASSED HERE WESTBOUND
THE MORNING OF SEPTEMBER 13, 1805.

CLARK WROTE,...."I tasted this water and found it hot & not bad tasted
...in further examonation I found this water nearly boiling hot at the
places it Spouted from the rocks... I put my finger in the water,
at first could not bore it in a Second."

ON THE RETURN JOURNEY THEY CAMPED HERE JUNE 29,1806
ENJOYING A HOT BATH AND FOUR DEER FOR SUPPER, THEIR FIRST
FRESH MEAT IN FIVE DAYS.

CLARK WROTE,.... "I observe after the indians remaining in the hot bath
as long as they could bear it run and plunge themselves into the creek
the water of which is now as cold as ice can make it.".

mounds that grew on a muddy bottom beneath very shallow water.

After those ancient rocks formed, they lay undisturbed until sometime between 70 and 100 million years ago, when the Rocky Mountains began to form. The main events in formation of our part of the Rocky Mountains happened between 70 and 80 million years ago; that was when the ancient sedimentary rocks in the mountains around the Missoula Valley were crumpled into folds. You need to look at a geologic map to see those folds, but you can see the evidence of their existence just by looking at the steeply tilted sedimentary layers in bedrock exposures.

Rocks in the northern end of the Bitterroot Range are basically similar to those in the other mountains around the Missoula Valley, except that they have been through more experiences, and they do look different. Those rocks were cooked at high temperature into metamorphic rocks, schists and gneisses. South of Lolo Peak, the Bitterroot Range consists of granite, an igneous rock formed by crystallization of molten magma, the ultimate in hot rocks. Baking of the metamorphic rocks in the north end of the range and crystallization of the granite farther south both happened between 70 and 80 million years ago, another aspect of formation of the Rocky Mountains.

No one is yet wise enough to

An exposure of Precambrian sandstone. All of the hard bedrock around and beneath the Missoula Valley is Precambrian sedimentary formations. DAVE ALT

be quite sure how old the Missoula Valley may be, or exactly why it exists. But there is no doubt that the valley has been here for some tens of millions of years, as much a structural part of the Rocky Mountains as any mountain range, a feature of the earth's crust. No river carved out this broad basin set within its surround of high mountains.

Some geologists contend that the Missoula Valley formed along with most of the other major structures in the Rocky Mountains. That would make it between 70 and 80 million years old, give or take a few million years. Certainly the valley is no older than that. Other geologists maintain that the Missoula Valley formed during a later spasm of crustal movements, that it may still have been forming as recently as 30 or so million years ago. Someday, we may know who is right.

Everyone agrees that the Ninemile fault defines the straight northern edge of the Missoula Valley, and must at least partly explain its existence. But informed opinions differ as to when and in what

direction the Ninemile fault moved. It might be well to point out here that the same fault continues straight west to define the northern edge of the Ninemile Valley, too. From a

geologic point of view, the Ninemile and Missoula valleys are one continuous basin that just happens to have different names at its opposite ends.

It also seems clear that the mountains along the southeastern end of the Missoula Valley—Mount Jumbo, Mount Sentinel, and on south down the east side of the Bitterroot Valley—are the trailing edge of the Sapphire block. That big slab of the earth's crust moved about 50 miles east into Montana between 70 and 75 million years ago. But it isn't obvious that the Ninemile fault and rear edge of the Sapphire block can by themselves explain the existence of the Missoula Valley. For now, we will just have to accept the existence of the valley, hoping someday to understand it more clearly.

The Missoula Valley certainly existed in essentially its present outline by about 40 million years ago, but it was at least 3,000' deeper then than now. During most of the last 40 million years, the Missoula Valley has been filling with sediment washed in from the surrounding mountains. That

The glistening surfaces on this exposure of Precambrian bedrock in the Rattlesnake Mountains north of Missoula were sheared about 70 million years ago, during the deformation that created the Rocky Mountains.

Ancient shorelines of a series of lakes held by ice dams in present-day Idaho still are evident in the different-color bands on Mount Jumbo.

exposures tell us something about how things were then.

Much of the Renova formation is soft gray clay that turns out upon closer study to be degraded volcanic ash. Most of that ash probably drifted in from the Western Cascades of Washington and Oregon. Those extinct ancestors of the modern High Cascades are the nearest major volcanoes that were erupting the right kind of ash at the right time. Horrendous eruptions there blew great clouds of ash into the air to drift east on the wind and heavily blanket the northern Rockies. Then rain washed the ash off the mountains into the broad valleys, where it stayed because that is where the streams dried up.

Meanwhile, the occasional heavy desert rains washed sheets of sand and gravel into the valley floor, interlayering them with the deposits of volcanic ash. Some of the rains spawned mudflows, another desert specialty. Gurgling porridges of thick mud studded with boulders poured down the mountain canyons and spread across the valley floor to interlayer with the ash, sand

happens if the climate is so dry that streams can no longer carry the debris of erosion out of the valley and down to the ocean, precisely the situation that now exists in desert places such as Nevada. Those 40 million desert years left their mark on our landscape,

and on the way we dwell in it.

Valley-filling sediments began to accumulate about 40 million years ago with deposition of the Renova formation, a thick accumulation of assorted debris well displayed in the roadcuts along Interstate 90. Close study of those and other

and gravel. Year after year those deposits piled up, thousands of feet of Renova formation sediments in the valley floor.

Many beds of gray volcanic ash in the Renova formation contain abundant fossil leaves of the Dawn Redwood tree, which still lives today—but not in places as cold as Montana. Those leaves suggest that the climate was fairly warm while the Renova formation accumulated, and not so dry that trees could not live on the higher mountains. The formation also contains numerous small pieces of petrified wood that could have washed down from the mountains, but no petrified logs or standing stumps to suggest that trees grew on the valley floor.

Even so, there were swamps here and there on the valley floor, just as there were swamps on the floors of mod-

ern desert valleys in the arid southwest. One of them left its record in Coal Mine Gulch, east of Grant Creek on the north side of the valley. A small mine there that produced coal for the local market more than 50 years ago went out of business because the quality of its coal was so poor—it made an appalling cloud of smoke and left great heaps of ash, while providing very little heat. But the stuff is coal, basically a solid mass of plant debris of the kind that accumulates in swamps.

Renova formation sediments now fill most of the valley floor. They are probably about 3,000' deep under the city of Missoula, thin to nothing around Frenchtown, but show up again to unknown depth in the Ninemile Valley end of the basin. Most of us would be just as happy without them.

The Renova formation is

about the worst kind of source for water. All that gray clay and those mudflow deposits are almost watertight. The beds of sand and gravel are, for the most part, too erratically distributed, too thin and too discontinuous to provide abundant or reliable sources of well water. Holes drilled into the Renova formation are more likely than not to be dry. Wells that succeed tend to produce grudgingly, and are likely to run dry after a few years. Without careful planning, that water stinginess of the Renova formation could eventually limit economic growth in the Missoula Valley. It has already caused great difficulty in several subdivisions on the north side of the valley, which were planned to depend upon well water.

When it gets wet, that volcanic ash degraded into gray clay swells up, acquires the tex-

ture and consistency of soft soap, and becomes just as slippery as grease. Slopes eroded on Renova formation clays tend to slide if the ground gets soaking wet. For various reasons that include septic tanks, lawn watering, leaking water mains, broken sewage pipes, and dry wells to dispose of surface water, residential development invariably tends to inject water into the ground.

Renova formation beneath the high benches on the north and south sides of the Missoula Valley presents a serious potential landslide hazard. The housing developments on the south-side benches don't have septic tanks, but do continue to inject water into the ground in other ways, as they have for many years. No one can predict when that water may accumulate to the point where sections of the slope will slide on slimy beds of water-saturated clay.

The potential for eventual landslides is probably far greater on the relatively undeveloped high benches along the north side of the valley. The last movements of the Nine-mile fault broke the Renova formation all along the northern margin of the valley, and steeply tilted its sedimentary layers. The large number of natural landslides on the benches along the north side of the valley testify to the instability of those tilted layers, to the potential hazards involved in building houses on them.

Some of those landslides are visible from the ground as tracts of lumpy topography. If you really want to see them, watch from the air the next

Big streams erode big valleys and can carry or move large boulders. At some time in its past Rock Creek has flowed with volume and force.

time you fly in or out of Missoula. Most appear not to have moved for a long time, possibly not since the climate dried out after the last ice age, but addition of water to the ground would probably start them off again. They will pose a threat to future housing developments along the north side of the valley.

The Renova scene ended about the middle of Miocene time, 20 million years ago in round numbers, when the climate became very wet and almost tropically warm. Red laterite soils like the modern red soils of the southeastern United States and central American developed on the Renova formation. Remnants of that red soil surface here and there on top of the Renova formation. Watch for occasional splashes of red in roadcuts and hillsides below the high benches, especially along Interstate 90.

You can trace those remnants of red soil west into the Columbia Plateau of eastern Washington and Oregon, where they show up as layers of red soil sandwiched between lava flows. Age dates on the

lava flows leave no doubt that the red soils are between 10 and 20 million years old. Old lake beds also sandwiched between the same lava flows contain fossil leaves of trees very much like those that thrive today in the southeastern United States. If the climate was wet enough then to support the kind of hardwood forest that now thrives in Florida, it was certainly wet enough to keep big rivers flowing through the Northern Rockies.

Imagine the Missoula valley with a broad river flowing through it, the familiar mountains covered with dense subtropical forest, colorful butterflies fluttering in the humid air. That was the picture for approximately 10 million years. During that time, the big river and its tributaries deeply eroded the Renova formation in the floor of the Mis-

soula Valley, carved its formerly smooth depositional surface into rugged hills.

A few remnants of the old Miocene stream valleys still survive in more or less recognizable form. The most obvious is Pattee Canyon, a broad erosional valley far too large for the tiny stream that now trickles down its floor. A large stream must have eroded that valley, probably during the late Miocene interval of wet climate. Except for the present, that was the only time during the last 40 million years when the climate was wet enough to maintain a large stream.

The Clark Fork River between East Missoula and Drummond flows through a valley that appears to be overly large, as does Lolo Creek upstream from Lolo. Remnants of what looks like an old bedrock valley floor appear as flat benches here and there along the valley walls of both those streams. Like Pattee Creek, both appear to have eroded their valleys into the floors of much older valleys eroded during the wet climatic interval of Miocene time.

The red stuff is laterite soil that formed under the wet and warm climate that prevailed during part of Miocene time. The gray material on top of it is gravel laid down during Pliocene time when the climate again was very dry.
DAVE ALT

Then, about 10 million years ago, the climate changed again, became, it would seem, even more arid than it had been while the Renova formation was accumulating. The lush hardwood forests and the rivers died in the drought. Then, during another 8 million desert years, occasional heavy rains swept in sudden torrential floods off the barren hills and into the floor of the Missoula Valley. Each flood left broad sheets of gravel on the valley floor.

One after the other, those deposits of gravel filled the floor of Pattee Canyon, filled the old valleys eroded into the Renova formation during the wet time, then buried the hills. Here and there they buried and preserved a few remnants of the red soil before it was all eroded off. Deposits of gravel finally piled up high enough to restore the valley floor to a smooth surface not quite so high as the original depositional surface of the Renova formation had been. We call that gravel the Six Mile Creek formation.

Recognize the Six Mile Creek gravel by its generally large pebbles and scarcity of clay and silt. Most of the gravel is brown, colored no doubt by red soil eroding off the hills. As in the Renova formation, all the pebbles come from local sources, which shows that no connected network of streams existed to bring pebbles in from distant sources.

The Six Mile Creek gravels generally lack plant leaves and pieces of petrified wood, probably because there is so little clay in the formation to provide good conditions for their preservation. Nevertheless, we can be sure that some plants did grow here then because the formation contains widely scattered bones of obsolete horses, camels and other animals related to the denizens of modern deserts.

Six Mile Creek gravel now exists in some places as a thin veneer on top of the Renova formation, in other places as deep deposits filling old valleys eroded into the Renova formation. Many of the gravel pits around the valley, including the big one at the mouth of Pattee Canyon, work those deposits. They are valuable sources of construction aggregate.

The occurrence of that gravel is erratic and its thickness impossible to predict because it buries the old landscape eroded onto the Renova formation. People lucky enough to drill a hole into a nice thickness of Six Mile creek gravel, perhaps one that fills an old valley, are almost certain to get a generous water well. If the drill misses a valley and penetrates an old hill in the Renova formation, chances of finding an ample water supply are not nearly so good. That is mostly a matter of luck because there is no good way to predict what the drill will find.

The climate again became wet enough to maintain a network of flowing streams sometime between 2 and 3 million years ago (call it 2.5 million). It is probably no coincidence that the shift to a wetter climate seems to have coincided with

the onset of the great ice ages. The two climatic events were probably linked, but no one can yet explain how.

Imagine the Missoula Valley, undrained for 8 million or so years, filling with water that had no place to go. A lake formed and rose until it finally overflowed through the lowest point on the divide. Then water pouring through the spillway eroded its channel deeper until it finally drained the lake. That spillway survives as the course of the Clark Fork River downstream from Frenchtown. Meanwhile, water overflowing from the Flint Creek Valley poured down an old stream valley left over from the wet interval of Miocene

time to establish the modern course of the Clark Fork between Drummond and East Missoula.

It seems that all the modern drainage of the Northern Rockies began flowing in that same way after the climate became wetter sometime between 2 and 3 million years ago. All the narrow canyons that connect the broad valleys of our region follow the spillways that formed as lakes began to overflow, one into the other, to establish a connected drainage net.

As soon as the Clark Fork and its tributaries began to flow into the Columbia, eventually into the ocean, they started the long job of excavating the deep deposits of valley-

fill sediments. The Clark Fork began cutting its modern erosional valley through the deep valley filling deposits of the Renova and Six Mile Creek formations. Now the flat part of Missoula stands on the floor of that erosional valley, and houses densely cover its slopes along Whitaker Hill and the South Hills. The flatter surfaces above those steep slopes on both the north and south sides of the valley are remnants of the old floor of the Missoula Valley that existed before the Clark Fork River began to flow.

Look at Mount Sentinel, a peculiar-looking mountain because two broad valleys in its crest do not continue down the slopes to the valley floor.

They just end. The elevation where those valleys end is about the same as that of the highest valley-fill sediments, the highest water-rounded gravel, on the benches north and south of Missoula. So it seems that the entire Missoula Valley was once full of Renova and Six Mile Creek formation sediments up to the level of those lost valleys in the top of Mount Sentinel. That must have been the level of the valley floor about 2.5 million years ago. Since then, approximately 800' of sediment have been eroded to bring the valley floor down to its present level.

It seems reasonable to assume that the rate of erosion in the soft valley fill sediments must have been vastly greater during the last 2.5 million years than in the hard rocks of the surrounding mountains. So erosion of the valley-fill sediments increased the difference in elevation between valley floor and mountain tops by about 800'. Our mountains look that much higher now than they did when the Clark Fork River began to flow.

Excavation of 800' of valley-fill sediments is only a start. To judge from known depths of such sediment in other western Montana basins of comparable size, it seems reasonable to suppose that at least 3,000' of Renova formation probably remain beneath the City of Missoula. That should last a few million years.

McCauley Butte, the isolated hill that watches over the Target Range area, was a spur of Blue Mountain 50 million years ago, before the Renova formation buried it. When the Bitterroot River began to flow in its present course about 2.5 million years ago, none of that hard bedrock was exposed—the river probably started flowing on the Six Mile Creek gravel. By the time the river eroded down through the Six Mile Creek gravel and the soft Renova formation onto the hard bedrock, it was well entrenched in its valley. That left it no choice except to carve the narrow canyon that now separates McCauley Butte from Blue Mountain. Meanwhile,

Top: The major notch on the right of Mount Sentinel marks the end of that little valley's deposition of materials to Missoula Valley. Since then some 800' of valley floor have been eroded. Left: McCauley Butte—cut away from Blue Mountain by the Bitterroot River.

89

erosion of the soft Renova formation exhumed McCauley Butte. So now it stands there in the open again, probably looking very much as it did before the Renova formation buried it sometime around 40 million years ago.

Ice age glaciers came and went time and again with very little direct effect on the Missoula Valley. Craggy peaks and deeply gouged valleys in the Rattlesnake Mountains north of Missoula, in the Ninemile Range farther west, and in the Bitterroot Range, show that glaciers inhabited those mountains. Lolo and Squaw peaks, two of our most familiar landmarks, are beautiful examples of glacial sculpture. But the terminal moraines that mark the farthest advance of those glaciers show that they never made it out of the mountains and onto the floor of the Missoula Valley, never got below an elevation of about 4,000'.

Had you lived in the Missoula Valley during an ice age, you would have seen those high glaciers maintain a glistening white cap on the mountains all summer. In all prob-

View toward Stuart Peak, Rattlesnake Wilderness. The Rattlesnake Mountains survived ice-age glaciers, which did not reach into the Missoula Valley.
GEORGE WUERTHNER

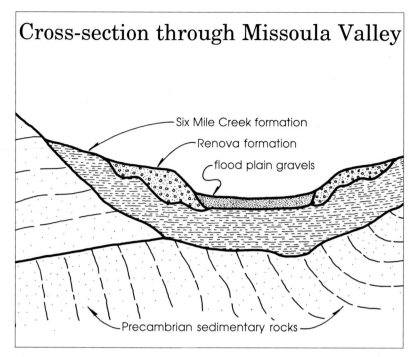

Cross-section through Missoula Valley

Six Mile Creek formation

Renova formation

flood plain gravels

Precambrian sedimentary rocks

ability, the climate was much wetter then than now, so you would have known a much bigger Clark Fork River than we now see. That wetter climate almost certainly supported a much heavier forest cover than now grows in the Missoula Valley. The place must have been about as nice then as it is now, until the creek rose.

The first geologist to write about the Missoula Valley observed in 1878 that glacial lake shorelines mark the mountain slopes. Those faint horizontal lines that show up so vividly on the lower slopes of Mounts Jumbo and Sentinel when the snow is melting are far too perfectly parallel and

horizontal to be anything but lake shorelines. Nothing in nature but the surface of a lake is perfectly horizontal.

It seems that ice age glaciers moving south from British Columbia through the Purcell Valley of northern Idaho dammed the Clark Fork River at the present site of Pend Oreille Lake. That happened about 15,000 years ago, very recently in the long history of our valley. The water backed up into the mountain valleys of western Montana to form an enormous lake, which, at its deepest filling, reached an ele-

vation of about 4,350', a volume of more than 500 cubic miles. So there were times when more than 1,000' of water flooded the floor of the Missoula Valley. We have a few souvenirs.

Icebergs and pack ice drifted in Glacial Lake Missoula carrying embedded rocks. Some of those rocks dropped from the drifting ice as it melted to settle through the lake onto its muddy bottom, others were stranded in places where the ice ran aground, then melted. Most of those dropped rocks now litter the eastern end of the valley and the slopes of Mount Jumbo and Mount Sentinel—those areas because the prevailing westerly winds drove the drifting ice to the eastern end of the valley. Look almost anywhere in the part of Missoula between Higgins Avenue and Hellgate Canyon for big, angular blocks deeply embedded in the ground—big rocks perched on the ground are merely part of a landscaping scheme. The angularity of those rocks shows that they were carried bodily to where we now see them; not rolled along because that

This block of Precambrian mudstone still rests where it landed as it dropped from an iceberg floating on Glacial Lake Missoula. DAVE ALT

would wear off their sharp corners.

Sediments deposited in Glacial Lake Missoula cover several large and small patches of the valley floor. The largest provides the flat surface for the airport. Watch near there for roadcuts in pale gray silt that tend to look very slightly pink on rainy or gloomy days. The rough terrain just west of the airport with all the closely spaced dry stream valleys appears to be an old badlands landscape eroded into the lake silts, then covered by plants.

Ice is not the material of choice for a major dam because it floats when the water behind it gets deep enough. When the ice dam that impounded Glacial Lake Missoula floated, it broke up into blocks of ice, and that was the end of the lake. But not the final end, because the glacier

continued to advance south out of British Columbia and again blocked the Clark Fork River, probably within a few years. There is certain evidence that the lake drained and refilled at least 41 times, good reason to suspect that it may have done so many more times.

Counts of annual layers in deposits of sediment laid down in the floor of Glacial Lake Missoula show that in 36 of those 41 fillings, the lake existed a total of just less than 1,000 years. The other five fillings would add a bit to that total. Something over a thousand years of flooding is only a moment in the long perspective of the Missoula Valley.

Of the 36 fillings of Glacial Lake Missoula for which we have a sedimentary record in the Missoula Valley, the first was the longest: 58 years. Then each successive filling

lasted for a shorter time than the one before, down to nine years for the last of the 36. It seems reasonable to assume that the lake level filled each year that each ice dam lasted, so the highest shoreline must be the oldest, as successive ice dams were smaller and lower. Evidently the glacier that dammed the lake was beginning to waste away, so it floated and broke in a lesser water depth each time.

And each time it broke, all those hundreds of cubic miles of water drained in a matter of two or three days, releasing the greatest floods of known geologic record. Estimates of the flood discharge down the Clark Fork River are in the range of 8 to 10 cubic miles of water per hour, greater than the combined discharge of all the rivers of the world. The greatest flood discharge ever measured on the Mississippi River was 0.02 cubic miles per hour.

A wall of water more than 2,000' high started from northern Idaho toward the present site of Spokane. Those horrendous floods scoured across eastern Washington, pouring

westward across the grain of the landscape instead of following the stream valleys south. The floods went down the Columbia River, where the water was more than 1,000' deep in some places. They backed up into the Willamette Valley of Oregon where floating ice dropped blocks of our distinctive western Montana bedrock. The Missoula Valley bears a few marks of those catastrophes.

The rush of water pouring over the notch in Mount Jumbo eroded two great basins in the crest of the ridge above Lincoln Hills. Meanwhile, the much greater torrent of water rushing through Hellgate Canyon scrubbed all the soil off the south canyon wall. Look sometime at the bare bedrock exposed above the old Milwaukee railroad grade. We see very little evidence of those sudden drainages in the main part of the valley because its breadth provided room for the water to move slowly. But look where the Clark Fork River again flows through a constricting canyon as it leaves the Missoula Valley below Huson. Big knobs of bedrock there tell of the sudden rushes of water that scrubbed the soil off the valley floor.

Except that the climate has dried out since the ice age ended, and the plant cover has probably changed, the Missoula Valley must look about the same now as it did after Glacial Lake Missoula drained for the last time. Look at the shorelines on the mountains. They are very faint, very shallow, yet they are there. If those shorelines on those steep slopes have survived the last 15,000 years, then so must nearly everything else their age. The Clark Fork River has carved some of the glacial lake sediment away, and the big angular boulders that the ice left may have sunk a bit deeper into the ground, but the scene has hardly changed. Change comes slowly in a valley that is tens of millions of years old.

Missoula Resources

City of Missoula
City Hall
201 W. Spruce
721-4700 (all departments)

Missoula County Courthouse
200 W. Broadway
721-5700 (all departments)

Historical Museum at Fort Missoula
Building 322
Fort Missoula
728-3476

Missoula Area Chamber of Commerce
825 E. Front St.
P.O. Box 7577
Missoula 59807
543-6623

Missoula Children's Theatre
221 E. Front
728-1911

Missoula City/County Library
301 E. Main
721-2665

Missoula City Parks and Recreation Dept.
721-PARK

Missoula Museum of the Arts
335 N. Pattee
728-4447

Missoula Senior Citizens Center
705 S. Higgins
543-7154

Mountain Line
721-3333

U.S. Forest Service
Missoula Ranger District
5115 Highway 93 S.
251-5237

University of Montana
Information 254-0211
Campus Events Hotline 243-2020
Field House Ticket Office 243-4051
Performing Arts Center Box Office 243-4581
Ticket Booth, University Bookstore 243-4999
University Center 243-4581
University Theatre 243-4581

Left: Champion International, Bonner; above: Missoula from south of Leisure Highlands, Greenough Mansion in foreground; top: Missoula Museum of the Arts.

*The Greenough Mansion from
Leisure Highlands.*